W9-CAA-620

RCollins
8/10/88

HOW SHALL I LIVE

HOW SHALL I LIVE

Transforming Surgery or Any Health Crisis Into Greater Aliveness

Richard Moss, M.D.

CELESTIAL ARTS
BERKELEY, CALIFORNIA

Simone Weil reprinted with permission from THE SIMONE WEIL
READER copyright ©1977 by George A. Panichas, published by David
McKay Inc., New York, NY.

The poem by Rainer Marie Rilke from POEMS OF A BOOK OF HOURS
copyright © 1941 by New Directions Publishing Corp. translated by Bab-
bette Deutsch reprinted with permission of New Directions Publishing
Corp.

Copyright © 1985 by Richard Moss, M.D.

Celestial Arts
P.O. Box 7327
Berkeley, California 94707

Cover Art by Wolfgang Gersch
Cover Design by Geoff Harris
Book Design by Abigail Johnston
Typography by HMS Typography, Inc.

No part of this book may be reproduced by any
mechanical, photographic, or electronic process,
or in the form of a phonographic recording, nor
may it be stored in a retrieval system, transmit-
ted, or otherwise be copied for public or private
use—other than for "fair use"—without written
permission of the publisher.

First printing, August 1985
Manufactured in the United States of America

ISBN: 0-89087-418-2

1 2 3 4 5 6—89 88 87 86 85

Table of Contents

ACKNOWEDGMENTS

Joan McIntyre for major editorial work and organization, as well as for friendship and laughter.

Anita Brown for additional editorial assistance and loving friendship.

Dixie Shipp for the title.

Judy Johnstone for final editorial touches.

In particular, I want to thank David Darrow, Mary Fisher, Bea Ledyard and my associates at Three Mountain Foundation.

Finally, heartfelt thanks to Patricia Carney, whose tireless support and selflessness continue to inspire and humble me.

DEDICATION

To all those—past, present, and future—
who have come to the edge of their being,
and, with no certainty where the next step
would take them, have gone forward into
the Unknown.

Introduction

Sometimes I go about
pitying myself
and all the time
I am being carried
on great winds
across the sky

CHIPPEWA INDIAN

THIS BOOK GROWS from my own experiences: as a patient, as a doctor, as a conference leader and as a spiritual teacher. It is about the relationship between healing and the transformation of consciousness. Writing it has felt rather odd, because the shift in consciousness that took me out of traditional medicine in 1976 so transformed my life that those years seem only a distant dream. Nevertheless, I am still drawn to the subject of health, not in the traditional view as a problem to be conquered, but as *aliveness*, for I have come to understand life in a new way.(1)

To me, wholeness is the key to aliveness. It is more than just physical vitality; it is radiance, coming from being at one with yourself and your experience. Life then flows through you and radiates from you. Aliveness is not necessarily about feeling better, curing ills or solving problems; it is about feeling *more*, being in touch with a larger dimension of awareness. When this happens, a new quality of life force animates you. The disorganized energy of ordinary consciousness becomes coherent and unified. We could call this a state of grace.

Over the years I have seen that, as they came to this sense of wholeness, many people who were ill improved dramatically. Others who later underwent surgery (or other medical processes, like chemotherapy) did remarkably well and felt their improvement resulted from an awakened capacity to become one with their experience. They could enter a deeper level of aliveness and enhance their life force even in the midst of crisis. In fact, *crisis made this even more possible.*

Occasionally there were healings that went beyond anything I could have believed possible from my traditional medical background.(2) These phenomenal healings and personal transformations occurred when people forgot for a moment about striving for health, growth, or understanding and became radiantly alive in themselves. One day I realized that there were numerous people approaching surgery, or another health crisis, who might welcome a book to help them focus on the larger potential of their experience—a book that would help them get well *and more.*

I thought this book would be easy to write, but it wasn't. The inner reaches are vast, and there is a great difference between teaching directly and formulating principles the reader can use. Trying to write simply and clearly, I found myself presenting the ideas in a way that denied their intrinsic paradox. This paradox was the most difficult hurdle for me, and I want to tell you about it.

Many books are written today about health. Most propose formulas involving exercise and diet; a few discuss attitude and love, and many prescribe meditation, positive thinking, and visualizations. All these things have validity and help people. Yet, since my awakening, I have had deep reservations about proposing any formula for health or healing. My experience has shown that while we often succeed in changing some aspect of ourselves through certain techniques, this rarely gets to the heart of the problem or leads to a new understanding of life. The key to deep change is not as much in our conscious control as we'd like to believe. Indeed, in transformational conferences, if there is a goal of any kind, the transformative potential (and thus the healing potential) is limited. While we can undertake methods for restoring health, we must not neglect wholeness, which involves a dimension beyond cause and effect—beyond the issue of suffering and what to do about it.

There is no formula for wholeness. Yet here I am, writing a book that could be taken as a formula for meeting crisis. In fact, we *can* prepare for surgery or meet other health crises in a way that increases the likelihood of healing. For me, this is the paradox. I appear to be defining a problem and offering a solution, and I know that if this book is interpreted that way it will lose its capacity to invite wholeness.

There is no way around this paradox; it must be embraced; it is a consequence of any invitation to growth, to adventure, and to change. Having acknowledged this, I want to share what happens for people as they make the journey to wholeness. The real transformational conference is life itself, wherever we are. Hospitals can be temples, and the dark moments doors to new potential, if only we will it to be so.

❋

A door opens wide when danger and death approach. Somehow when we no longer feel in control, we become available to a deeper aliveness. Perhaps we realize how little aliveness there had been. Before my awakening I courted crises because I intuitively recognized the peculiar gifts that accompanied them. But seek them or not, life provides such moments anyway. Any experience can be a transformational door. Wholeness stands ready to greet us at any time. It longs for us as we long for It. Yet we often hang back until there is no choice. Health crisis may not be the best door to a larger potential, but it *is* one that almost all of us will eventually face, and its multidimensional possibilities should not be wasted. These times are among the greatest doors for awakening us to vastness and the wonder and mystery of life. To face health crisis fully is really an affair of the heart and an invitation to our highest potential. We can shift to a higher energy wherein the very sense of existence is more connected to others and there is a greater capacity to love. And this process of shifting to a higher level of energy is integral not just to health, but to the whole domain of human relationship.

In our society the expansion of our spiritual and social awareness is essential to our survival, and what we do with the potential energy of a transformational door like health crisis is crucial not only to ourselves, but also to our world. We are all concerned about life on Earth; we all know we are standing on the brink of thermonuclear disaster; we all want to heal the world. However, we cannot save our world at our present level of consciousness. We must shift to a higher level to see that the world is already whole, so that we can begin to live that reality. Thus, any episode in our lives that expands our consciousness contributes to the potential wellness of our world. *From a hospital bed, it is possible to contribute to the healing of the planet.*

Each year, more than 19 million people in the United States face a potentially transformative event in the form of surgery.[3] More than 19 million of us will have our flesh cut open; we will have tubes inserted in our veins and down our throats. There may be weeks beforehand to prepare for this event or only a few hours. There may be weeks or months of recovery afterwards. During the actual surgery, we will give ourselves over utterly into the hands of others. We may never have done anything like this before. We may face family and friends for the last time. To a greater or lesser degree, depending upon our conscious preparation, we will be changed by this experience. When living and dying approach each other, they teach surrender in a completely new way. Such an experience can have a tremendous impact when approached consciously and consecrated to wholeness.

This book is based on the experience that *health and our state of consciousness are inseparable.* We may think of our bodies as basically mechanical. But this is only partly true. Our bodies are consciousness; we are energy systems. As we shift consciousness and the energy of our life becomes more radiant, our bodies and spirits are renewed and "enwholed." *Enwholing* is a word I have coined to describe the process by which we fall into a state of wholeness and become at-one with ourselves, each other and the very moment. Letting go when we have done all we can do is the very heart of enwholement.

Such a transformation is never accomplished alone, especially when it is centered around health crisis. It requires sharing with our family, our doctor, our nurses, our teachers, and our friends. This sharing maximizes the aliveness of everyone involved. It is not the same as the ordinary social or professional exchanges of daily life. It is a sharing that expands and lifts consciousness, and for many it must be learned.

Even if your family or friends don't know anything about energy and have never thought about life in this way, they may be open to new ideas during a time of health crisis. Together you can call on love and offer it to the healing process. It requires an attitude of non-emotional affection and a willingness to risk being open. Everybody is a source of aliveness and love that they can bring forward if they are willing to enter the deeper harmony of life, and lay aside their hopes and fears for you.

❀

Early in my internship I discovered a walnut-sized, hard, immobile lymph node in my groin. Cancer loomed strongly in my awareness. I spent a month facing the possibility of major illness and even death. I was stunned to see how powerless I felt. After a period of observation, the node was biopsied and found non-malignant. But a change had been wrought. Nothing mattered as before. Never again could I deny my own mortality.

I began to suspect that the greatest limitation on our capacity to be whole is the fear of death. To go beyond this fear meant transcending the basic sense of identity, the ego. (The word *ego* is used here to refer to that personal sense of "I am" that separates me from thee, demands my comfort, defines my boundaries, insures my safety, and so on. The ego is the champion of personal reality. It is an energy system that defines the body-mind and even our sense of spirit. As long as this basic energy system remains fundamentally unchanged, consciousness, including health, remains separate from a larger potential.) I had participated in various kinds of therapies and self-growth processes, traditional and non-traditional, and I knew they could not take me beyond my personal reality. They could help me modify ego patterns, but could not alter the forces that create the ego. When these explorations were exhausted, I began to shift naturally to a transformational perspective.

At first , I remained within the familiar framework of being a doctor. I added meditation, prayer, energy sharing and diet change to my formula for health. But, most important, I began to share more deeply with my patients. As I asked more of myself, I began to ask my patients to do more than just get well. Gradually I realized that the arena of traditional medicine was too small for my continuing exploration. Missing was the space for the intuitive elements of consciousness: the capacity to just "be," to enjoy life because I am, because I exist, and to feel this as a sense of holiness and wonderment. It meant trusting a deeper creative force that might allow something new to enter. It was no longer enough for me to take some of the techniques for developing awareness and apply them to the old life. I had merely been embellishing my basic ego structure and had not really faced the new. Something else was needed; in a word, it was *undoing*.

I realized medicine had allowed me to remain immature in the sense that it provided the meaning and motivation for my days, much like a parent provides structure for the child. It defined my schedule and the reasons for my actions. I could feel very adult and very important, and I was serving others in a valuable way while having many profound experiences that taught me a great deal. Yet I knew that I was enfolded in a cloak of convention, which I had donned without ever recognizing myself as a free man. How could I possibly help my patients go beyond their own ego-sustaining structures when I had never looked beyond mine? Children can't help children to be adults.

The prospect of living more fully from the immediacy of my own being—whatever that was—was wonderfully exciting and intensely frightening. My whole life up to that time had been like a narrow shaft of light, illuminating only a portion of life. Somehow I had to expand the shaft into a full radiant pool of illumination. I knew intuitively that if I didn't give myself fully to this process, the potential for transformation could just as easily take the form of disease, perhaps cancer this time. The warning of a few years before had never left me. So I set aside my career in medicine and began to move in a new direction.

Today I know that the transformational perspective complements and fulfills traditional medicine; it does not reject or compete with it. Traditional medicine cannot be denied, but it grows out of the rational elements of human consciousness. Therefore, it is not complete in itself. If traditional medicine and, for that matter, most holistic approaches could be likened to a graph with an X and a Y axis, X might be called the Problem and Y the Solution. Within these two dimensions, there are many possibilities that do succeed in giving us "health" of a certain quality. The transformational perspective adds a third axis and a new dimension; thus it reveals an infinity of new possibilities. The nature of this new axis is the process that occurs as we transcend our basic orientation to life by falling into our immediate experience. This frees healing energy from areas where traditional medicine and therapies don't even know how to look.

This book is divided into three parts.

Part I. Beyond Health and Healing, describes the transformational process and the basic principles for heightening energy that can help maximize the transformative and healing potential of a health crisis.

Part II. Some Personal Stories, includes my own experience of surgery and expands on the ideas in Part I. The cases illustrate the principles and show how self-healing is not separate from traditional medicine.

Part III. Doors for Greater Awareness, invites the readers into a creative participation with their bodymind. It is both playful and serious. The chapters in this section explore important nuances of awareness and show how, by creating contrast to our usual consciousness, we can begin to learn from our own bodies. The exercises can generate higher energy states and greater aliveness. Thus they help prepare for surgery, for cancer treatment, or for dealing with any other health crisis. Indeed, they can maximize the transformative possibilities in any life crisis. This section brings the potential of transformation into daily life, particularly in the realm of transmuting energy – the shift from one level of consciousness to another. In this way, we can free energy bound in one state (for instance, fear or confusion) and make it available as aliveness. These exercises can also act as doors to new levels of experience or provide experiential bridges to explore what we may already be sensing intuitively but have been unable to interpret clearly for ourselves. At the end of each exercise is a Commentary that augments the exercises, provides additional examples, and forms an important part of the text.

If you are going to use this book to help you heal in a medical crisis like surgery or cancer treatment, you need courage, support and energy. You must take charge of the process because you are the one who is approaching the transformational door. You must decide for yourself, both with your intellect and with your whole being. If you are too ill to read, ask a friend to read this to you. Discuss the ideas and explore the exercises with each other.

Read the book with both your heart and your mind. If you come across something you do not understand with your mind, ask your heart.

RICHARD MOSS

Part I

Beyond Health
and Healing

1 . THE TRANSFORMATIONAL PROCESS

God speaks to all individuals through what happens to them moment by moment.

J-P DE CAUSSADE
The Sacrament of the Present Moment

THERE ARE FORCES AND EXPERIENCES in life that lead us to explore ourselves more deeply and change the funda-mental beliefs upon which our lives rest. To speak of the trans-formational process implies that the heart of our nature can change from the illusion of separateness to a growing sense of unity with existence and our fellow man without sacrificing our individuality. It is more than how we think or what we believe, for it involves the very life force that animates us. Transforma-tion is not an "alternative." It does not lead us out of this world with all its physical, financial, and psychological concerns.

Rather, it brings us into this world. It makes possible a more immediate and sensitive relationship to life as it is.

Most of life is concerned with going from A to B to C. If A is where we are when we are 20 years old, then B will be where we are when we are 30, with the new house and young children. And C is where we will be when the children have left home and we can travel again. But this linear progression from A to B to C is only one aspect of the change we experience in life.

Another aspect is the transformation of consciousness, which can be described as a movement from A to A′ to A″. An individual at A is able to look at life from one perspective. Without being aware of it, he or she is controlled by certain fears and desires. But this same individual at A′ recognizes that those fears are either imagined or that they grow out of a narrow view of one's own nature and the nature of life. At A″, one has transcended the previous limits, and there is greater understanding of oneself and mastery of forces like emotional reactivity. There is less fear of loss, for A″ has joined life and its infinite energy. The degree of freedom and the capacity to relate to life available at A″ may make the individual nearly unrecognizable to those who knew her or him at A.

The movement from A to A′ to A″ is like a sphere whose radius grows larger with a consciousness embracing an ever-expanding reality. This expansion is a kind of hallowing in that what already exists acquires greater significance and meaning.

At A, certain values and needs determine our way of life, while at A′ these things are no longer as important. Prior to my own awakening, the only experiences that had significance for me were those of the greatest intensity. Thus I loved to climb mountains or to work in a busy emergency room. On the other hand, doing the laundry was boring—activity to be gotten out of the way so I could get back to "real life." Life was intermittently exciting and fulfilling with long gaps of emptiness in between. In contrast, hallowing is the spherical expansion of the moments of fullness into all areas of life. The gaps become smaller and smaller and finally disappear altogether.

After the first awakening, my new sensitivity was so acute that all of existence was charged with an indefinable aliveness and my old patterns of self-stimulation were so transparently crude that to engage in them was like trying to squeeze my being into a tiny box. When the light on the leaves is as meaningful as an intense mountaineering experience, a rapturous love affair or a jealous emotional conflict, the latter gradually fall away as the central focus of one's life. I still climb mountains occasionally and I enjoy sensual intimacy but, whereas before, these were like a drug taken to fulfill the addiction to intensity, now they are part of the richness of life and have no more or less significance than writing or doing the dishes, which are equally as gratifying.

The transformative moment from A to A′ to A″ also could be described as growth from one capacity to love . . . to a greater capacity to love . . . to a still greater capacity to love. *Love* here refers to that quality which feels its relationship to a larger wholeness in the midst of any experience. Movement from A to A′ implies a greater capacity to love because one's being at each successive level is more fundamentally in relationship to all of existence.

Transformation implies a refinement and extension of the radiant energy or aliveness that permeates one's being. It is as though, as you move from A to A′ to A″, there is a successive refinement of the personal self, which becomes more substantial, more a reflection of life's intrinsic wholeness, and simultaneously more ordinary. Just by being, you radiate a presence that has physical, mental and spiritual impact upon all those about you.

As the energy heightens, the significance of the individual expands. At A, the person is an individual with very personal concerns and needs, the center of which is the family structure. At A′, the "individual" senses his collectivity. At this level, each of us is an "I" that is "We"—a reflection of humanity as a whole. Finally at A″, the "individual" ceases in any personal sense and knows himself to be identical with Life or the Whole. Illumined spiritual teachers, such as Christ and Buddha, are examples of individuals who have realized themselves at A″ and who then brought the message of freedom, brotherly love and compassion into the theatre of human life.

The movement to A′ means greater aliveness. With each refinement of the energy, there are subtle bodily changes, and these changes are the key to health in general. For example, while a man at A has a body that works within a certain range of probabilities, the body at A′ works within an expanded range of probabilities. Therefore, the rate of healing at A is different from the rate at A′. At the higher energy state, you may bleed less when cut, recover more quickly and require less medication, etc. At A, food is consumed out of necessity or pleasure. At A′, food has so much impact on consciousness that it can feel like a drug. Thus one becomes very sensitive to diet, not out of self-interest or fear, but because our consciousness is the instrument through which we radiate the Divine.

Food can augment or refine our energy, or it can ground it. If we want to expand and refine, then fasting or a vegetarian diet is good. This diet tends to make our energy less dense, more expansive and open. Fasting and vegetarianism have long been associated with spiritual work. In reality, diet has little to do with spiritual development; it just makes possible a certain movement in energy that, in turn, shifts the quality of awareness. This shift provides a contrast to our usual state. As we change our diet, to some degree we change our perception of reality. It is not that we see a better or more spiritual reality, just a different one.

Is there a special diet for approaching surgery or for attaining greater health? Since changing one's energy level will change consciousness somewhat, it may also result in modifying health. For example, a radical dietary change such as the Gerson diet or macrobiotics can produce such a change in one's energy that the body can sometimes heal itself. But this change depends on many factors. There is no formula that is right for every person. Generally, if you tend to be a very dependable, stable, rational, self-contained individual, then a vegetarian diet may make you more available to heightened levels of consciousness, and this may improve your health. If, on the other hand, you are highly sensitive and easily influenced by your environment, so that it is hard to maintain your own centeredness, then a heavier diet that includes meat may help you center more fully on yourself. To open up and become more available to the shift from A to A', fasting and a vegetarian diet may be helpful, but once the shift has occurred and you are learning to handle new levels of energy, there are periods where large amounts of protein, and food in general, are required.

Evidence suggests that when we undergo a physical trauma, good nutrition is very important. But the body is also a reflection of consciousness. Diet is important, but even more important is our overall state. Most of us eat out of habit, unaware of how food enables us to tune ourselves to greater awareness. Unconscious dietary habits support a lower energy state, and even if food were "nutritious," it still could limit health. It is not so much what you eat as *how* you eat. Eat with gratitude. Be aware that the food you consume is going to be used by your whole being to fulfill your highest potential. Release any sense of conflict about food, especially the kind that grows out of the various notions about the right and wrong things to eat. Begin to trust your intuition. It is not so much what you put into yourself, but how you receive it.

Similarly, one must be aware that medications, like food, effect us in accordance with our level of energy. At A, a drug will have its expected result, but at A', a quarter of that amount may be nearly overwhelming.

At A', there is a softening of body armor, a translucency to the skin, a tremendous increase of sensitivity as the body becomes an instrument of more open relationship with existence. At A', sex may no longer be experienced as genital and can occur as a merging through the breath or a glance. These are only some examples of alterations in the bodily nature accompanying the radiant transformation of consciousness. It is important to be aware of the differences between A and A′ in order to understand that nothing about us is fixed. We are energy systems. By exploring the transformation of consciousness, we also transform our bodies, for consciousness and our bodies are inseparable.

❀

While we remain in the A to B to C level, our concern is, "How can I get well as quickly and painlessly as possible so that I can return to the life I know?" But our search for healing is likely to remain within the same system that brought about the disease in the first place. While we may alter the disease with traditional medicine and surgery, we rarely come to its root. The very "me" who wants to heal my disease is the "me" in whom the disease developed. Therefore when we say, "I want to be healed" (particularly if we say, "You heal me") we're really saying "I don't want to change. I want to preserve 'me.'" The disease says, "No, you can't preserve yourself." But we keep on insisting, "Save me, preserve me!" If one can release the identification with "me," the disease will modify according to the depth of this release. In a sense, both transformation and disease kill us! Disease takes us out of life, while transformation kills the familiar identity by making us bigger.

In life, there is always the possibility that we begin to shift, not from A to B to C, but to the understanding that each event moving us (A to B, B to C) can likewise be regarded in terms of its capacity to move us A to A′ or B to B′. At A′, our whole idea of health and disease may change, and we may realize we're not so much interested in health/disease as we are in wholeness/aliveness. And once we begin to shift our awareness to the perspective of wholeness, we discover we are moving towards good health.

❀

Again and again, I have observed that the efforts and concerns of ordinary consciousness have very little impact on healing. It is the shift of consciousness that precipitates the healing process. The conscious mind only witnesses that process. A simple example of this is the cut finger that heals without the apparent participation of the conscious mind. If the conscious mind did have to take over and achieve the healing of every cut, we might bleed to death. Every cell in the body unfolds without conscious awareness. Through reading books, learning techniques, and doing visualizations, the conscious mind can modify what it perceives, but it can't heal and it can't make us whole. Thus the involvement of the conscious mind is only effective if it turns us towards wholeness and encourages us to yield to a higher possibility. We can then perceive the transformational potential of every moment and offer ourselves to that.

In fact, the way of radiant growth requires us to cease our usual efforts. For, while we try to control our lives, we are limiting our energy relative to a larger possibility. The consciousness at A is elastic; it will expand and contract within a certain range of energy, but no conscious intent can permit transforming to a wholly new level of energy, because such a shift represents a leap into the unknown. To the conscious mind, this seems like death. Faced with this possibility, the reflex is to preserve the "me." All our efforts to save ourselves resist the transformative movement from A to A'. But there will come a moment when we understand the limits of conscious effort and learn to let go of even our most sacred attempts. This letting go, when combined with the intuition of a higher possibility is the essence of genuine spiritual practice. It is at the point when our own efforts relax that a deeper force can act through us and reveal a new consciousness. Often the jump to a new energy will occur when we are weakened. Thus it is in moments of crisis, a health crisis in particular, that the door to transformation may be opened to us.

2 ❧ UNIFYING SELF AND EXPERIENCE

The most beautiful music of all is the music of what happens.

OLD IRISH TALE

IF YOU WANTED TO GIVE GOD EVERYTHING, the only thing you could give would be your present experience of who you are. *Thus the door to God, or to our own true nature, is our experience of the moment.* And that door opens when we and our experience become one. When this union occurs, consciousness jumps to a new level. It is the moment of greatest awareness and aliveness, the moment of transformation. Since these doorways often appear in the midst of painful and unhappy experiences, transformation implies great courage. Jesus, for example, became profoundly unified in the midst of intense suffering.

On a more personal level, a good example of the unification of self and experience is the moment of orgasm. If we separate ourselves from it by analyzing, it is lost. Similarly, the athlete who must think of each step as he performs falls short of excellence. This is the purpose of intense training—so that at the right moment, we will function as a whole without thought. If an athlete achieves this, we are awed. When a team performs with such unity, the energy released is tremendous. This energy release is what attracts huge crowds to professional sports events.

As we fall toward ourselves by being present for whatever happens in life, we become unified. In this state, we are at our highest energy. All performers are reaching toward this unified state of being, and it is why there is an almost spiritual aura surrounding a great star. Many of us have been deeply moved by a singer whose abandonment to the song touches something so profound in us that we experience an altered state of consciousness. Audience and singer merge in the larger energy. The popular song "Killing Me Softly" speaks eloquently to this.

Unifying self and experience means becoming more and more centered in the present moment. We must pass through fear, ambivalence and doubt into the simple wholeness of whatever this moment is. It means moving beyond the consciousness that says, "I want/I don't want what's happening to me."

When we've stopped reacting and are centered in our experience, we are no longer separate from the doctors who will reach into our bodies or from the tools and chemicals they use. Nor are we separate from the bed in which we lie. The hospital becomes a temple where we release into the vastness of our nature. But to reach this point we must unite with our fear.

It is very hard to reconcile fear and pain with wholeness. The first reaction is to flee. Fear exists because we are defending "me" at some level. F.E.A.R.: Forever Evading Another (larger) Reality. The moment we let go of the "me" who is afraid, we are no longer divided in ourselves, no longer separate from the fear, and it ceases to be. Instead we discover that when there is no longer any separation between ourselves and the moment, fear becomes a highly energized state that can be experienced as emptiness and peace. As long as we unconsciously insist on maintaining the "me," there will be fear, especially when we face transformational potentials such as surgery. If we find a way to avoid the fear or to overcome it, we have learned to manipulate reality, and to empower our egos, but we have not gone through a transformative door. To enter the fear directly is to expand the parameters of the self. This is what is meant by going through the door of fear. In essence, it is necessary to embrace death. Such a radical willingness connects to the deeper energy that empowers transformation.

Transformation brings us to a realm of energy beyond our instinctual habits. The transformational perspective is that of a lover who does not attempt to control the beloved. On the contrary, this lover seeks to merge with the beloved. In the transformational process, life is our lover and we seek to merge with it. It is not enough to manipulate life for our needs and desires; it is equally exciting to honor how life is living us. We are not only the sculptor, we are being sculpted. To appreciate this, we must begin to expand the boundaries of our understanding and cease our narrow judgments of what is whole or healthy. The real breakthrough occurs at the moment when life is truly realized as lover, and when we see that we are already whole. This is, I believe, the healing power of what is called Christ Consciousness.

To flee from fear in all the ways our culture offers—socializing, watching television, problem-solving, denying what we feel, looking for comfort, and on and on—means we are falling out of love with life. We are running away from ourselves. It is this splitting of our consciousness that decreases the energy so vital to realizing our full potential. At a certain point, all this must be set aside. We must consciously realize that we do not know anything and become available to life as it is. Even if this is painful, still it must be done. Just as the whole is greater than the sum of its parts, so we in our wholeness are greater than we realize. While we lie in psychic pieces, the result of our flight from the intensity of Now, we postpone and limit our capacity to heal.

3 ✿ HEIGHTENING ENERGIES

EXPLORING TRANSFORMATION over the years, I found a key insight began to reveal itself. As suggested earlier, the phenomenon of heightening energies is greatest when we are unified in the moment. However, the depth and quality of the energy available depends on something of which we are less aware. This is what I call *consecration*.

Consecration is our relationship to the mystery of life. It is the question we ask our hearts and attempt to answer through our lives. More than an attitude, consecration has to do with how life reflects the sacred, that intrinsic aliveness that is beyond understanding. At the deepest level, consecration is not subject to the will. In this sense, it could be called the soul's dedication, and it changes (or rather, we live different levels of consecration) as we mature. However, we can choose to consecrate ourselves to life in a particular spirit, and this choice, especially when it begins to reflect the soul stance, has the greatest influence on the direction and quality of our transformation.

In multidimensional reality the realms of experience at every level (physical, mental, psychic) are infinite and there are infinite bodily activities we can invent, infinite ideas to develop and apply, infinite sensations of energy, infinite visions and mystical trances, infinite ways we will want to change our lives. Nearly every possibility implies a different aspect of ourselves. For example, some relationships encourage our optimism, while others tend to bring out our insecurity and possessiveness. Business dealings may reveal our aggressiveness or distrust, while a summer storm or the evening light may arouse our sense of wonder. If these ever-changing reactions are all we know of ourselves, what, if anything, guides us when we face the unfamiliar such as surgery and are ready to let go? The answer is not known although we can call it grace. Nevertheless, there is something in the way we approach the transformative moment that seems to determine where it leads. This approach to the sacred is the consecration. It is the central theme, the golden thread, that is our relationship to Consciousness itself.

❀

Ask yourself now, "What is my life consecrated to?" Let the answer come as a feeling deep within your heart. It may surprise you.

❀

Few of us are ever aware of our deeper consecration until it is revealed to us by life itself. Usually we sense this deeper connection in scriptures or in historical accounts of the lives of great souls. Perhaps we have met someone who has realized Oneness and inspired us. Something inside us hears a deeper message and recognizes its truth. There is a yes in our hearts and without even realizing it our consecration has begun to change. But, no matter how we come to the recognition, the more fully we know ourselves, the more our conscious consecration and the deeper stance begin to converge and harmonize. To me, this convergence is the essence of enlightened living and of health.

As we grow spiritually, our consecration begins to join us to

Wholeness or Oneness. In a subtle way we begin to feel we somehow belong, and that life is our lover. It becomes hard to be aggressive or pushy because our deepest feeling is of the intrinsic unity of life, and we don't care to propound one aspect of life over another. We begin to develop the attributes of equanimity, surrender, humility, and humor. In the ordinary world, this may appear as weakness and passivity. But actually it is the development of the inner strength to meet the unknown, which is very different from the strength needed in ordinary life.

Early in life, our unconscious consecration is to the basic sense of separation rather than to wholeness. Because we appear separate, we feel vulnerable and we explore being powerful, manipulative and "successful" in the conventional sense. Quite unconsciously, our consecration reflects our fear of life, our sense that life is dangerous, that it must be managed and controlled. This is a developmental phase in our growth. We are developing our basic identity, our sense of "me." Thus, at this point, our life is consecrated to developing the "me" sense, the ego. And, just like the Whole or the One, the ego is also sacred.

Each of these aspects of the sacred imply an entirely different relationship to life, and very different levels of energy. Thus as our consecration shifts from "me" to the One—which includes both the individual as separate and the sense of uninterrupted wholeness—the basic ego structure shifts and we begin to access energy in a new way. It is as though in the earlier stage we only access energy through our own activities and this requires something to push against, something to be separate from. Later, as we begin to shift toward wholeness, we access energy through a surrendering of ourself into existence, so that we lose ourselves at the egoic level and discover a new Self. This is essential with regard to health because we must learn to access energy not only through the separate self, but also through our wholeness. So much of disease is the struggle of both individual and collective humanity to make this shift and to develop a corresponding lifestyle.

As you approach healing, the energy available when you are

just trying to get well (consecrated to "me") is often far less than it could be, for it is not the whole of you that participates. Thus, the bodily enwholing does not reach its full possibility. If you realize the narrowness of this ego-dominated viewpoint and can let go unconditionally into your experience, trusting in the fundamental wholeness of every moment, a higher energy becomes available. When you are consecrated to the highest potential beyond the conventional sense of healing and are willing to let go into the intrinsic wholeness of life, there is no longer the feeling of being involved with something lesser or wrong. Then the door of surgery or chemotherapy may become transformational. Likewise, if everyone with whom you are involved is equally consecrated, the potential becomes greater.

But, once again, consecration is not something to be applied like a formula. From the perspective of heightening energy, not everyone can open unconditionally into the moment. You can't give away what you haven't got, and a person who has not deeply developed the "me" must not yield himself prematurely. Thus some individuals must make a very full and powerful statement of "me" that appears to be quite untrusting and controlled, rather than surrendered.

When we speak of heightening energies and being consecrated to the highest potential, we can speak about openness and love in some and selfishness and belligerence in others, and we are talking about the same process! Medical statistics have demonstrated that frequently the belligerent, uncooperative patient has a better prognosis (particularly in cancer) than the agreeable, cooperative one. Clearly this is an observation about aliveness and not a recommendation for a particular kind of behavior. The highest potential is our fullest aliveness and not some idea about what it is to be a good person. It is not until we have given ourselves permission for that greatest aliveness, no matter what the form, even if it involves rage, selfishness or downright nastiness, that we can fulfill our highest potential. Some individuals are developmentally at the point where the consecration is rightfully to "me." Anything that empowers this "me," that creates fuller aliveness, is in harmony with the deeper consecration even if it is not socially acceptable, or "spiritually" proper. But this energy, once allowed, must be channeled creatively. It must become a clear statement of what one wants and how one is going to go about getting it.

To use rage to move into a sense of power and aliveness may be quite appropriate. If that's true for you, don't hold back; let that energy come through fully. Eventually you will move to the next step and use this energy to meet your surgical experience as a lover. Then you can, with full inner authority (and not merely passive agreeableness and acquiescence) begin to offer yourself in a new level of consecration and realize a more profound level of wholeness. A person who has fulfilled his personal power can begin to surrender it to the Divine power without compromising the integrity of his own development. Whereas someone who makes the gesture of surrender because it looks good is fooling himself and will not arrive at his fullest energy potential.

❀

Consecration and its relationship to the transformation of consciousness is difficult to explain. I have come to understand it only partially as, over the years, I watched people go through transformational experiences. It seems that being unified, being in the state of oneness, being at the highest possible energy should always lead to an A to A' shift. Yet, this is not the case. Why do so many people transcend themselves in so many different life experiences and rarely undergo transformation? Why doesn't an athletic event like an Olympic downhill ski race produce a transformative state of oneness rather than a transient peak experience? One transformational conference participant had been a U.S. Olympic skier. During the conference, he came to a level of such tremendous energy that he couldn't close his hands; to him, they felt as if flame were pouring from them. He began to sob uncontrollably. The only time he had ever experienced a similar energy was in the starting gate of his downhill run during the competitions. After that experience, he had lived a good life, but he felt that he would never again know that kind of aliveness. He was sobbing because he had found another way to reach a similar aliveness. But, most important, he was crying because he realized that this aliveness had always been available. All he had to learn was to open unconditionally into the present moment.

If we can touch the moment when we are not skiing, but being skied, we have gone through a door into a unified state and a higher energy. But the transformative potential is limited by our consecration to "me:" It will be the energy available in a self-possessed, self-fulfilling activity; it will be the energy available through competition, through a fundamental dynamic of separation. It will be bounded by the basic ego structure and thus will not reveal something that is beyond that. Furthermore, even as we let go, it is in a thoroughly defined context. We may not know what will happen. If it is a battlefield we may not know if we will survive, but we always know who or what the opponent is and why we are there.

Despite the intensity created from the sense of separation, this energy is far less than that which occurs when our consecration is to something beyond our own self-involvement and fundamentally unknown. At best, the context into which we release can be intuited but not known directly while we remain in the separate "me" dynamic. Thus, letting go into the unknown is the essence of transformative process. It has a greater enwholing potential than letting go within a known context like surgery or any medical treatment just as a cure.

If our consecration implies an open perspective, then our understanding as we go through a door of unified awareness will tend to be more universal, inclusive and penetrating. Thus our consecration becomes the single most important thing to which we must give attention in any process of transformation, especially when we are concerned with health. In all the cases of radical healing of which I am aware, a consistent theme appears. At a certain point, they all let go of their narrow personal involvement and become aware of the largeness of life. At the moment when these shifts occur in their consecration from "me" to the Whole, they are not separate from their experience. They have become unified. Thus our conscious consecration can point us toward a possibility, but it has little power to change us until the moment of let-go. Then, it is possible that the sense of "me" and the sense of the greater Whole can become united. This is the transformational moment of greatest significance. It is also the moment of deepest healing.

As life emerges moment by moment, it is our consecration that enables us to allow the unexpected. To consecrate our lives to the highest is to reach beyond comfort into the fullness of a reality which we cannot necessarily predict, a reality where the best insurance policy is laughter and the unshakable knowledge that, no matter what, the riches available to us are infinite. But beneath any conscious consecration, there is always the deeper consecration, and it is this we must discover. When we finally realize the deeper consecration directly, a new relationship to everything and everybody becomes possible. Life becomes abundantly full and effortless.

4 * CONSCIOUS RELATIONSHIPS

HUMAN BEINGS CAN AUGMENT or siphon off life energy in themselves and in others. In fact, energy exchanges happen between people all the time and reflect the fact that we are intrinsically inseparable—the I that is We. Thus, heightening of energy is inseparable from how we relate.

I have found groups to be one of the best settings in which people can heighten personal energy. In transformational conferences, healing consciousness is available at every moment. It is not a problem-oriented consciousness. Thus, in these conferences, it is important to move toward relationships that create aliveness in the moment and not to try to resolve the questions people have about their health. When people enter a unified state together, tremendous energy is present. Group energy is far greater than an individual can achieve alone. When people come into unity within the group energy field, their experience of wholeness is immense.(4)

To fall toward the center of oneself is profoundly energizing. When many people are simultaneously exploring this, the phenomenon is further enhanced and can transform bodily processes. A seriously ill man with a brain tumor attended one of my conferences right after completing radiation therapy. The first few days of the conference he could barely walk from his bedroom to the conference room, a distance of thirty yards. He was exhausted. But by the fifth day, he climbed the mountain behind the ranch, a two-thousand-foot elevation gain over several miles of cross-country walking on rugged terrain. The difference between this man upon arrival and five days later shows how heightened energy restores health. The man eventually died, but for a period of time he had more vitality and well-being than he had had since the disease. (The exercises in Part III of this book are adapted from some of the energy heightening processes utilized in the conferences.)

While the heightened energy of the conferences resulted in many healings, it must be said that some people did not appear to improve. Entering higher energy states in a transformation of consciousness is not a panacea. After exposure to a higher energy there is often a difficult period of adjustment and integration, and one has to learn to be ordinary. The challenge to grow in consciousness is so great that people often turn from it, preferring, perhaps unconsciously, to let their changes happen more gradually. Even illness can be easier to deal with than the transformative breakthrough, because in illness the personal self can remain intact. While we may not like being ill, at least we think we know what we are dealing with.

Though you may not be able to attend a transformational conference, you have a ready-made group in the form of your family and friends. Under the usual conditions of surgery and hospital stays, the family acts as a support system, but a support structure is different from a real source of energy for one who is ill. As a support structure, the family can get caught in conventions that dissipate focus and energy. If they try to protect you from their feelings, or if you protect them from yours, you are in a state of separation based on ideas and convention. This is inevitably a low-energy situation.

Gossiping, talking about the future, or reminiscing about the past are safe and familiar ways to relate. However, these same activities disperse energy and limit the closeness and communion that is possible between people. It is natural for your loved ones to be afraid of losing you, and likely you are also afraid. But by refusing to deal honestly with what is actually happening, you are simply supporting each other's fears. To heighten the energy within the family support system, these fears must be faced.

Issue an invitation. Ask your family and friends to stop socializing and, instead, to open their hearts. Suggest that they center in their highest potential rather than in what they want for you. (If a relative or friend visits you in the hospital and does attempt to inspire you to live or get well or whatever, he or she may be adding to your problems by blocking some deeper process in you. With all good intentions, this person may miss the opportunity to unite with you, so that both of you miss the door.)

Ask your family to join you in the immediacy of the moment. They may confess that they are afraid of losing you or vice- versa. They may open themselves to you by telling you how frustrated they feel because they don't know how to help you. Whatever you both say and do, such honesty and love can unite you in the moment. There is more energy in this than in hiding or pretending to be cheerful and positive.

Suggest to your family that they release their preconceptions about how you're going to heal, about how long it will take, and about how it will happen. Ask them to make their presence available to you. Ask them to touch you. (It doesn't matter that you are not at your most glamorous or that you may feel downright ugly.) Don't let them stand at the front of your bed, a respectable distance away. Most people are afraid to get close, so you'll have to find a way to communicate your need without being trapped in the drama. If you yourself are afraid of this kind of closeness, don't withdraw. Move toward your fear. You have to let go of yourself to go through fear. And you have begun the very process that will heighten your energy and thus prepare you for surgery.

In learning how to tap the group energy from within your own family, you become a soul on a journey, not just the beloved mother-father-sister-brother-spouse-friend-daughter-son. Neither are you "the one who is sick." Bring your family together in an energy-sharing ritual. (See Door 5, The Energy Embrace.) Gather them in a ceremony of hand-holding, praying together, sitting quietly and sending love to you. Teach them that they can radiate love, care, and energy through touch. Ask them to drop their self-consciousness and just be present.

During the surgical procedure itself, your family and friends can meditate. Ask them to unify and "sense into" a direct relationship to the whole experience, including the medical people who are caring for you—the doctors, nurses and orderlies. (See Chapter 7, Life as a Lover.) In this way, you can offer your family and others around you a creative way to contribute to your life.

Find a way to unify with your physicians and healers. Call upon them to make the same commitment to their highest potential that you yourself are making. Your biggest responsibility is to yourself. If you're nasty and difficult, you may be heightening your own energy, but you're pushing others away from you. It is necessary to find a way to augment your own personal aliveness and to tap the tremendous energy potential available when those around you can commune with you. When the people with whom you are working realize how deep your inner commitment is to life in its totality, they will be drawn into making a similar commitment themselves.

When a physician and the entire health-care community are challenged by the love and radiance of a patient to move to a higher consciousness, miracles can happen. Note that I said "challenged by love" and not by anger or criticism. When a healer feels he is being looked at deeply, with respect and compassion and not with need, he becomes humbled and inspired and draws closer to the patient and to the universal source of well-being. And when the healer sees that the individual with whom he is sharing has sacrificed superficial defenses and senses the transparent vulnerability with which the patient is entering into the healing experience, he is moved within himself to a greater depth and presence during work. One physician told me of a patient who had inspired him in this way. He said the woman was so honest, so direct, and so vulnerable with everyone that for the first time in his own life, he felt somewhat shabby and superficial. He had to go home and clean up an issue of integrity with his wife before he felt he had the right to operate on this patient.

It is difficult to be intuitive and sensitive while you are ill. But so much of the weakness is a result of never letting go fully into your wholeness (which is uninterrupted even in illness). From the unified place that doesn't resist illness or fatigue, you can access unlimited energy and it will shine from you. Share it with your doctor and your nurses. Reach out and touch them gently with your eyes, your words, and your hands. Don't forget that you are, first and foremost, human beings. When you come into direct rapport with another, there is greater love and everyone becomes more whole.

A good physician becomes a gifted artist in an atmosphere of love. The key is communion, the unification of the self, and the building of an energy field between you and your doctor.

❀

The transformational moment occurs when we lose ourselves. We must be willing to let go of what we want and raise the energy of our consciousness. Energetic rapport with others is one of the most direct ways to do this. We must go beyond familiar relationships with family, friends, and health-care personnel and open ourselves to a deep and unobstructed level as we invite others to do the same. To prepare for surgery, or just to bring ourselves to an optimum level of well-being, involves an understanding of how to fine-tune our energy. This is not a magic remedy, as if we could reach some level of energy and be free of all suffering and disease. While a higher level of energy often resolves a problem—even a physical illness—new challenges face us as the energy becomes finer.

We are more than what we seem to be. Our bodies are physical and obey biological laws, but these laws (such as the rate of bleeding or how much pain we feel from a particular kind of injury) change as our consciousness changes.

Any time we open ourselves more deeply to each other and to something that inspires us and expands our vista of life, our energy will become more alive.

Part II

Some Personal Stories

5 . MY OWN EYE SURGERY

> It is in affliction itself that the splendor of God's
> mercy shines, from its very depths, in the heart of
> its inconsolable bitterness. If still persevering in our
> love, we fall to the point where the soul cannot
> keep back the cry "My God, why hast thou for-
> saken me?", if we remain at this point without
> ceasing to love, we end by touching something that
> is not affliction, not joy, an essence, necessary and
> pure, something not of the senses, common to joy
> and sorrow: the very love of God.
>
> SIMONE WEIL

ONE DAY, WHILE I WAS DRIVING across the
Golden Gate Bridge, a strong impression grabbed my awareness. Now was the time to have my wandering eye repaired. It
was late 1978 and I had recently returned from a period of traveling in Europe, the Middle East, and India. The travel had

shown me the transformational process as it is explored in other cultures, and had, of course, been transformative in itself. I had resumed my work from a much deeper place and the last thing on my mind was my eyes, but the impression was clear and insistent. So there I was, realizing that I was going to have surgery some time in the near future.

My eyes had troubled me since childhood. I had tried eye exercises without much benefit, and I had not been willing to have surgery even though the opthamology department in medical school had strongly advocated it. At that time, the thought of eye surgery sent a wave of panic through me, and I hastily decided my eyes were not such a problem after all.

Actually, I had excellent control over the eye movement and did not suppress vision.(5) Therefore, although the problem was extremely limiting when I was tired (and even the smallest amount of alcohol produced double vision) I had lived with it well enough. When I was strong and well-rested, I could hold the image normally, and when I was unable to do so, I had learned to squint or to completely close one eye. The drifting eye was a direct feedback mechanism that showed me when I was relaxed and in tune with life, for even to be slightly out of tune produced more difficulty seeing.

Crossing the bridge, I recognized that the earlier fear was not merely the fear of pain: it was the fear of being a patient. I had entered medicine because I cared for people, but also I was unconsciously afraid of death. Medicine became a way to approach death and maintain the illusion of control. But as I continued my exploration of consciousness, I encountered the fear of losing control and the fear of death at deeper and deeper levels. Now this dynamic no longer barred me from the process of fixing my vision. However, I had discovered the positive benefit of my eye disorder as a feedback mechanism for my state of consciousness. The concentration necessary to maintain a fused visual image provided me with a kind of meditative skill. From early childhood, no matter what I was doing, another part of my awareness was always conscious of my eyes, squinting one or the other, or angling the position of my head to minimize double vision. Quite outside any conscious intent, I had developed a neutral witness, an attention that ran parallel but remained uninvolved in my activity. This witness was of tremendous importance in setting the stage to integrate the awakening process, for it allowed the dispassionate observation that carried me into a process of spiritual maturity. Without the witness, I might have been swept up in the intensity of the experience. Even as early as medical school, some part of me realized that the full benefit of this "meditation" should not be interfered with by medicine, for I had not yet become fully conscious of its significance. But once the witness faculty had become conscious, the eye problem was no longer necessary and, in fact, was a waste of energy. It was time for repair, and surgery was the most direct route. But I had no idea what a tremendously valuable experience the surgery would be in itself.

I had participated in many surgeries. However, except for my biopsy and other minor procedures, I had never been a patient. The eye surgery was expected to last about forty-five minutes to an hour. I personally requested local anaesthesia and was informed that this, combined with nitrous oxide, was preferred. The benefit of nitrous oxide as an anaesthetic is that during the operation the patient can be brought rapidly back to consciousness and can confirm the correction. So all the arrangements were made, and I concentrated on preparing myself for the long-avoided event.

Now picture this scene. You're strapped down on the operating table. You've been in the hospital for a day, and you haven't eaten for about twelve hours. There are brilliant surgical lights glaring overhead and your eyelids are retracted so there is no way you can avoid the blinding light. You are nearly perfectly conscious. Granted, you are not *supposed* to be conscious, but somehow you are! You can see the scalpel poised above you as the surgeon prepares to make the first incision. Potentially overwhelming, yes? But that is precisely the situation in which I found myself as the surgery began.

It is quite possible that the nitrous oxide was only partially effective because, as a result of the awakening, I had learned to enter states of altered awareness far beyond that produced by this level of anaesthesia. During the surgical procedure, I discovered I could stand outside the anaesthesia in such a way that my conscious awareness—the ability to observe the experience and comment upon it—was remarkably clear. The problem, however, was that while I was able to do this, I also lost much of the benefit of the analgesia and experienced excruciating pain. Surgeons, I found, don't like patients who are in intense pain. At times we can't help ourselves. We howl and yell!

The surgeon and the anaesthesiologist were highly skilled in their fields. After all, being a physician myself, I had sought out the very best surgeon for this procedure. The problem, if we are to call it that, was that I was unusually aware, so aware that I was able to watch the smoke drift up into my field of vision after the approach of the cautery, and hear Bach gently playing over the Muzak system, and to know, at the same time, that a surgical team was cutting and repositioning the insertion of "my" eye muscles because I had asked them to. I had thought that the experience would be a blur of unreality. All my personal preparation had been for the period prior to the actual surgery: I had released all conflict in me about the procedure as I became aware of it. I spent the day before entering the hospital alone, in silent retreat. I had re-explored the option of eye exercises to be clear that I was not inviting intensity when a program of responsible, gentle discipline would work as effectively. I became convinced that surgery was the most appropriate method. All my business affairs were in order so I had as much as two weeks to recover if I needed it. My friends had shared energy with me the day before in the hospital and were meditating during the procedure in order to join the process on the inner planes. Now, contrary to my expectations of dim oblivion during the process, I was still lucid. The freedom to scream and struggle, to rip myself free of the restraints and flee from the operating table was within my power. The realization of the physical destructiveness to "me" of such behavior gave me a moment of panic. Then, moving within, I remembered that I had invited this experience and there was nothing to do but release into it.

I found myself observing at many levels. The very idea that the eyes were pulled out as far as possible, that the muscles are exposed and severed from the positioning which has been theirs from birth and then repositioned seems uncanny. The fineness of the tools and the deftness of the technique are products of infinite, immeasurable evolution. The whole procedure sounds miraculous, and it is a miraculous gift of technological advancement. Yet, it is also primitive in a whole other sense. The primitiveness has to do with the way we relate to each other: for instance, the separateness of the health practitioners from the patient and from each other. There is just no conscious understanding of how deeply interrelated we are. I had understood our interconnectedness after my awakening and it became the basis of my conference work. But never had I appreciated so clearly the primitiveness of human relating and the implication of what was missing in medicine until that surgery. I was caught in an unbelievable paradox. It was miraculous and primitive simultaneously. It was important to me to remain present and alert. I had the choice of drifting into a dreamlike distortion and withdrawing from pain or entering a state of extraordinary clarity and perception with exquisite pain. I chose to remain in direct awareness.

The intensity of my pain demanded that I continue to surrender into the experience, releasing my reaction to the pain at deeper and deeper levels. I would check back into my body and relax the muscle tension that would creep in as the pain mounted. I regulated my breathing to maximize the effect of the nitrous oxide and to center myself so I wouldn't become overwhelmed. Movement beyond even this level was possible; for a time I was unusually aware of every sound, and of the physical location of everyone in the room through "feeling" their presence and emotional states. This had happened to me when meditating, daydreaming, or working, but this was heightened by the intense stress of the experience. My sense of vulnerability, and of being consciously surrendered into the hands of other people, was profound. I passed in and out of a state of awareness in which I understood universal pain, what it offers and how it controls us. For brief periods this became a timeless silence beyond pain.

When I would ask the surgeon how it was going, he would reassure me. And his words relieved both the pain and the tension far better than the nitrous oxide. When he took the time to answer me sincerely, a wave of great warmth would move through me, and I would be at peace. This did not happen when the surgeon talked with other members of the team, nor when all were silent—only when he spoke directly to me. When I asked him too frequently for feedback, he would turn to the anaesthesiologist and ask, "Doctor, is the patient getting any anaesthesia?" There was impatience and a little fear in his voice. I told the surgical team that my awareness was my own responsibility, and they should get on with doing the very best job they could.

Then the surgeon asked for a particular instrument. He asked for it a second time and, after a pause, a third time. With each request his voice became more demanding and a tension came into the room. Simultaneously, my discomfort increased. All of a sudden, a sharpness came flinging across the room followed by the sound of metal bouncing off the wall. In a fit of frustration the surgeon had thrown away the incorrect tool. At once my pain and fear increased tremendously. If they had known how open to them I was, they would never have allowed such an incident to happen. The nurse assistant would not have let herself be distracted by her personal problems (as I "knew" she was), and the surgeon would not have resorted to impatience and petulance. I told them what I was thinking. There was dead silence. I was scaring them. My cries had not daunted them, but my degree of sensitivity to the situation did. I decided to remain silent for the rest of the procedure.

After the surgery I sobbed deeply. The surgeon placed his

hand over my chest, and again I could feel a warmth flowing into me which helped me release once more. I sensed he was not aware of his effect upon me, but that this release was essential for my recovery.

I was not crying for myself. I was crying because millions have suffered such pain with very little compassion to help them through. I was crying for how few there are who have been sufficiently prepared to use such experiences consciously to deepen and mature. I was crying for how far medicine has come—that so much of the pain can now be mercifully avoided with drugs—but at the price of our sensitivity. I was crying because, without deeper awareness of Oneness, we unwittingly continue to inflict pain on ourselves and others even when we want to help. I was crying because pain and wholeness need not be brothers. I knew that I would no longer need pain to show me love. I had gone through a door.

The discomfort, nausea and other side effects of the anaesthesia, and of the whole experience, lifted abruptly with this flood of understanding, and I was suffused with an inexpressible sense of reverence and peace. Friends who joined me afterwards in my room were carried up in it and enriched it with their presence.

The surgical correction was superb. Even in the midst of it I was discovering a deeper level of life. Had I become too involved with fear, anger or helplessness during the whole process, had I refused to remain present and alert, had I not had the centering skills and a larger perspective, I could not have experienced such a deep sense of compassion for all life. Less aware, I might have been swept up in fear or anger and been unable to stand outside the anaesthetic stupor. By releasing the emotional and personal level of involvement and by letting-go to a deeper participation with the experience, a truth came. The very energy of it was the resolution of a whole part of my life as well as the inspiration to go deeper. It was for me a powerful healing.

Today, as I contemplated this experience, I asked myself a question and allowed myself a one-sentence answer: If I had the opportunity, what would I say to health institutions, to individual health practitioners, to anyone asking about health and life? I would say we must have a direct realization of the sacredness of our work and of ourselves. The one thing that can change our health-care system and our whole relationship to each other, make surgery more effective, and stimulate the entire healing process, is the direct realization of the spiritual dimension that unites all. Medicine, in fact, the whole human endeavor, must never be separate from the process of recognizing the True Self. To know the divinity of our own being even for a moment, to know we don't know, to release toward wholeness at those moments when everything inside us wants to shrink away from life, and to consecrate all of our work to this truth—this is what we must do. Then there would be no question of attention during surgery—no preoccupation with personal feelings, the schedule, or tomorrow's problems.

The surgical team operating on me had commitment and a mature technique, but no understanding of their capacity to participate with an energy so profound, so loving and enwholing, that it is even a kind of anaesthesia for the patient. The nurse would have known, *before* the surgeon requested it, which instrument he needed and where it was. A kind of reverence for the miracle and mystery of what we all were doing would have united us, and they would have received a great blessing—the knowledge that one's work and life are a singular whole, the very reflection of God.

Instead, each person was participating out of a separate space. Each had his own plans and his own needs. While this is natural, it does not allow the unification of conscious energy so vital to empowering the maximum healing potential. In many ways I was a unique patient and thus could observe the group energy as it tended to unify or disperse. And in many ways I was responsible for the lack of greater unity and mutual sensitivity.

At that time I was still cautious about expressing my personal experiences to fellow physicians. I had not risked their rejection by asking them to enter into deeper rapport with me and each other. I had prepared myself wholeheartedly; I had utilized the supportive energies of my friends, but I had not yet appreciated how important it is to involve the medical community in this process of unification and support.

It took my own surgery to show me how vital all the relationships are. We may not be able to do much to change our immediate circumstances but we can do a great deal to change how we approach life and one another. Our suffering must be redefined by our understanding of growth. Many more could be lifted up, and all of us along with them, if we began from a sense of the wholeness of life rather than the conquest of pain when we enter the healing process.

You may feel I am a unique person with special capacities and that you cannot participate in your surgery as I did. Perhaps that is true right now, but only in degree. My experience gives you the option to go a little deeper in yours. We do not need to reject fuller aliveness when it is offered because of the anticipation of failure or shortcoming. We can take the risk to go a little bit deeper, to continue to grow and to learn in ways which we didn't know before.

Often we don't understand the positive side to our illness. The concept of secondary gain is fairly well known. It refers to an unconscious motive for illness, such as the attention received from loved ones, or the ability to get out of a job we really don't want. But, in this sense, secondary gain is seen as manipulative and neurotic. The secondary gain in my own example suggests another dimension. Certain faculties of awareness were being developed, although I was not aware of it until, in a different phase of life, these faculties were suddenly very important. Diseases can be forces for change beyond learning greater patience or changing a lifestyle. Sometimes (and perhaps all the time) there is an aspect to the disease of which we are completely unaware. Sometimes we are being evolved for a higher possibility. Simply to eliminate disease without learning (at another level) what deeper process it may be calling us to means we will probably require some other form of suffering—perhaps another disease—to learn what is necessary.

It can be said that I was not facing a life-or-death situation. My suffering was mild compared to some. Undoubtedly it is easier to be wholehearted with elective eye surgery than it is with mandatory open-heart surgery or a colostomy that results in wearing a bag for defecation. I acknowledge this. Nevertheless, the potential of growth in another dimension is available to everyone, whatever the circumstances, if they have made some inner preparation.

As I entered that surgery, I had to surrender consciously and open myself on a deep level. The day before the operation I began to develop all the symptoms of an upper respiratory infection. The surgeon had warned me that if I had a cold he could not operate. Serious complications, perhaps even blindness, might result. But there I was, the day before, with a runny nose and chest congestion. Intuitively I felt this was a psychosomatic "cold" arising from my own subconscious resistance to letting-go into something so new and unknown. Before any deeply vulnerable process, I often had bodily reactions. The depth of the reaction often anticipated the depth of the coming experience. Even knowing this, I couldn't be sure it wasn't a cold. I very much wanted to go forward with the surgery, but knew it would be bad judgment to do so while ill. I had created a "damned if you do, damned if you don't" situation. It was that very conflict which intensified my awareness and energy prior to the surgery. But I also knew that the moment of transformational shift occurs when, with no certainty as to outcome, one surrenders. Once I committed myself to the surgery, the cold symptoms disappeared.

In my observation of the transformational process, we tend to create this kind of approach/avoidance crisis whenever we are at the threshold of a deep change. Being able to let go and really surrender into our experience becomes crucial here, providing we have consciously offered ourselves to the highest possibility.

When life has brought us to such moments, for whatever reason, they should not be wasted. The understanding of the higher potential that can awaken through such situations must be fully considered to be a part of health care.

6 ✲   SHARING WITH EARL

What lies behind us and what lies before us are small matters compared to what lies within us.

RALPH WALDO EMERSON

AFTER I LEFT TRADITIONAL MEDICINE, a few of my old patients tracked me down. In an average week, I saw two or three of them, as well as a sprinklng of new people. Many came hoping to find an alternative to traditional medicine, which they feared and distrusted.

To prepare for their visits, I would simply sit down quietly and allow my mind to become empty. Whereas before I would have boned up on the case, now I allowed myself to drop all assumptions about the visitors and what I might offer them. Then, when they arrived, I saw that it was possible to go into very deep states of rapport and achieve a profound understanding of the nature of their problems. But even more important was my appreciation of their basic wholeness. It was this sense of wholeness that had to be tapped. For nearly all of these people, medicine had helped them define and redefine their problems. But when a problem is defined, so are we—and always in a part of ourselves, never in our wholeness.

All I was doing as I sat with people was listening for wholeness—for that space where their energy seemed to be most available—and feeling when the separation between us fell away. When their concerns lacked real depth, their words felt hollow. When they began to speak more from the center of their being, a quality of richness appeared. I learned that it is not just content that communicates. Far from it! Underneath the words there is a vibration that creates a sense of presence. The presence is a much truer guide to the essence of our being than our words. When our plans and insights resonate with this fuller energy, we are connected to deeper levels of ourselves; we are more whole.

Perhaps the most important thing I learned as I listened from this state of meditative attunement was that a person in confusion and pain could be closer to the core of himself (and therefore closer to his fullest potential) than someone else who appeared self-assured. Clarity and assuredness aren't in themselves adequate indicators of a greater aliveness. Indeed, they may indicate a controlled, low-energy state. On the other hand, fear and confusion are often present when a person stands at the very edge of deeper being and doesn't know it. Clarity that comes from directly realizing a deeper wholeness carries a different quality. There is a sense of space, presence, and multidimensional availability. Even the peace some people feel when they have "put it all in God's hands" can be a very low-energy process. I realized that, for many, surrendering to "God" was just another form of denial. In our attempt to avoid uncertainty, confusion, and anxiety, we often take a path of lower energy. While too much confusion and anxiety is exhausting, and can even be a defense against moving into a fuller energy, it may be a door we must go through to reach a deeper state. My being in the most receptive energy state possible facilitated an automatic high-energy state in my visitors. This process, which is known as *induction*, led me to understand that at the level of the deeper energy we really are one body. The greatest gift I could offer was my own wholeness.

I saw that the deepest aliveness didn't make distinctions between traditional medicine and holistic treatment or between daily life and spiritual life. The traditional medical or surgical procedure is as much a part of the mystery of life as anything else and is a true door to wholeness. In its present form, it is also a new door, one that is here because of the way we live today. We are always trying to get rid of threatening doors: grief, uncertainty, pain, death, disease. Often we succeed. But a life without doors is too one-dimensional to encompass the depth and mystery of aliveness. Invariably, as we attempt to get rid of old ones, we create new doors that are at least as difficult to go through: complex surgery, chemotherapy, acid rain, genocide, nuclear holocaust—the list seems endless. The German mystic poet Rilke regarded modern man as a dark fortress, the windows shuttered, the drawbridge pulled up. To this image he whispers, "Don't you sometimes wish for the enemy?" The "enemy" is any experience that has the capacity to let in the light and open us to the mystery of life. In such an experience, we have to acknowledge, finally, that we don't know anything, that we never did, and that we are not in control. Being out of control is unbearably frightening for most of us; we are forever protecting ourselves. Doors were needed in the past as they are today and the way through is the same then as now. We must stop running away from the immediacy of what is, *whatever* it is.

Free to explore in new ways, I discovered new territory. I did not have to defend or recommend any particular healing approach. I found that energetic aliveness is something beyond reason. By staying open and moving toward the sense of aliveness, a presence filled these sharings. (This presence is hard to describe for it feels like love, but with no personal focus as the object.) Within it, the discrete sense of Body-self dissolved into a molecular aliveness and fears seemed to lose their significance. When this sense became so rich that it seemed palpable, we had arrived at a moment of understanding that opened the door to a new realm beyond the right or wrong, good or bad of any experience. From this awareness, all possibilities facing us are part of the wholeness of existence. Once we know this, a sense of meaning and a course of action become clear.

Some of the sharings went on for a day and then resumed the next day, if we were unable to arrive at this state of unity and clarity together. To me, this place signaled that we had come to a resolution or, more aptly, a new beginning. Our sharings began from a state filled with rationalizations and concepts, moved through states of fear, pain, confusion, and need, and culminated somehow in a sense of sacredness.

One of these early sharings involved a man, Earl, who was scheduled to have surgery to remove a benign tumor that had spread to the middle ear. Earl was a good-looking, up-and-coming young advertising executive. At thirty-five, he was bright and independent. He had attended a few personal growth workshops and had read many books on health and spirituality. He was certain there must be a better way than surgery to heal himself. He was convinced he had given himself (was responsible for) the disease and therefore was responsible for the cure.

As I listened to him, I sensed he was dispersed and fragmented. He had not considered the possibility that surgery could be a springboard to greater fulfillment, and not necessarily something to be avoided. Like many facing a serious illness for the first time, he had not explored his ideas about healing nor how his particular healing might occur.

In all, I must have seen Earl three or four times. During the first session, which lasted four hours, he spent the time verbally rambling around in his problem while I just listened, sensing towards the moment when he began to touch a deeper energy. He described his sessions with his doctors, his symptoms of facial paralysis, dizziness, hearing loss and the spread of the tumor. He was confused: One part of him saw the situation as a simple biological event for which he had no responsibility; another part believed that we create our own reality and was therefore questioning how he had created his disease.

I expected such an inquiry would lead to greater understanding and deeper aliveness, but I found the energy of his voice becoming less substantial. He was full of ideas about what was real and what was right. He offered one explanation after the other about his problem, but somehow there was no aliveness. He was moving in the wrong direction. Gradually there came silence. It was still somewhat contracted, but there was more presence than when he had begun. He left the first session intrigued and a little baffled. He wanted to come back, but he didn't know why.

In subsequent sessions, it became clear that what he was really asking for was some way out of his double bind. He recognized the necessity of the surgery because his symptoms continued to worsen despite all his efforts. Yet, could he accept it? If he admitted that he needed surgery, then he had failed to heal himself. He had created an either/or situation in which self-healing or natural healing was on one side and surgery was on the other.

Earl's dilemma is not unique. For many of us in similar circumstances, our greatest fear is choosing a direction, then committing ourselves wholeheartedly. We invariably find ourselves in some kind of polarization between alternatives, afraid that we are not acting as responsibly, maturely, or intelligently as we can. Usually the choices represent different aspects of ourselves and in neither choice do we feel whole. Illness makes us realize that we have been unaware, perhaps too passive, and not a full participant in our lives. We've been trusting to chance, afraid to look at ourselves. All of a sudden, we discover that we are ill and require surgery or powerful medications. These treatments become the symbols of our passiveness or lack of self-worth, and we reject them. But we know that we can't *really* reject them, so we grudgingly accept our fate and resentfully turn over our authority to traditional medicine. Or perhaps we play the flip side—blind and passive acquiescence.

Obviously, neither acquiescence nor resentful acceptance is a wise choice. Some sense this, and project a unified or higher possibility onto an alternative or non-traditional approach, particularly if it has a spiritual flavor. Like Earl, most of us have not faced this conflict or have opted for one side over the other. Current belief systems compound the problem: The body is physical and obeys mechanical laws, or the body is a manifestation of spirit; man creates his own reality, or what will be, will be. Psychologically, these beliefs may comfort us, but they prohibit us from reaching our highest energy. It's not that they're wrong. It's that the conclusions we draw from them are erroneous. The transformational door exists when we fully enter our experience beyond these beliefs. No one can touch the full potential for healing by believing that one treatment is good for the body but in conflict with the soul, or vice versa; or that one approach will prove him or her right and another wrong. The fact is that the fullest potential exists when the inner consecration and the outer action unify.

Earl's perspective shifted as the energetic induction of the sessions began to open him to another quality of awareness. He couldn't explain it, but he was changing. He began to see that he wasn't separate from his doctor, that healing was a process in which he was the "head" and the doctor was the "tail" of the coin. The healing potential resided in the wholeness of both together.

As his perspective widened to include the possibility of surgery, he began to experience subtle energized states of awareness. At the end of each session, just before we would stop, the room would become electric with presence. He would smile and say that he didn't know what we were doing, but it felt right. I never asked him to spend time with me. He would simply call up and say things were becoming clearer and ask if he could see me again. One day he realized that surgery was not essentially any different than any other life experience. Certainly, it promised to be an intense experience, but at last he had reached the place where it had become a valid option, something he could choose to undergo—or not. In fact, the real issue wasn't "aye or nay" to surgery, but whether he could remain as open to his own deeper aliveness during surgery as he was now. He actually began to look forward to surgery. He had shifted to a larger perspective.

For Earl, surgery had been a kind of unsolvable riddle. As long as it was approached from his usual level of consciousness, he was in terrible conflict. Whatever direction he chose, he was facing the death of a large part of his self-image and beliefs. He had created a "damned if you do, damned if you don't" situation. This necessitates a transformative shift of consciousness for it signals that we have reached the limits of our capacity to encompass our experience. It is a kind of psychological death/rebirth, a dark night of the personality. If we face it fully and let go into the dilemma with the sense that there is a higher but unknown dimension, we may well experience a basic transformation.

When we face death, at any level, we face what appears to be the end. All our presumptions about reality become useless, for they cannot take us to the unknown. Usually we repress the unknown by continuing old ways of coping. Perhaps the favorite of these is identifying a problem and then trying to solve it! We split ourselves into pieces, and then cleverly put ourselves back together again. Ultimately, death does not oblige such intellectual or psychological maneuvering. Death becomes an invitation to let go into the intuition of life's prior wholeness, to develop another kind of consciousness that I refer to as *wholehearted.* This consciousness is new and unfamiliar. But it makes possible moments of greatest unity and leads to higher energy. "In order to arrive at what you do not know, you must go by a way, which is the way of ignorance. In order to arrive at what you are not, you must go through the way in which you are not. . . ."(6) When Earl had reached the point where there was nothing more to discuss, a stillness filled the room and I concluded the session with a short ritual of energy sharing. I set up a table and had him lie on his back. Then I attuned myself to the finest possible universal energy and allowed it to flow through me to him by placing my hands just above his body. (See Door 5, The Energy Embrace.)

Three weeks after our last visit, he phoned to tell me about the surgery. The process had been called remarkable by his doctors. When they came to give him pre-operative sedation, Earl was so calm that he suggested he did not need it. They agreed! As he was rolled through the hospital corridors, he felt a joyous rapport with the orderly who was wheeling him. The elevator up to the operating suite made him laugh. He was like a child on an adventure. When he entered the operating room and looked at the people there, he was filled with a sense of loving gratitude. He said he was reminded of how he felt when he finished one of our sessions together. He insisted he wasn't "trying" to feel anything. "It just kept happening."

His surgeon reported that the entire procedure had been very unusual. As fast as tissue had been cut, the bleeding had stopped of itself. He had lost virtually no blood during the operation. Furthermore, his recovery was extremely quick and painless. Almost casually, Earl mentioned that the entire experience had changed him. While recovering in the hospital, he decided to begin a new career. He felt clear. In the unified state in which he met the profound stress of surgery, something had happened. I could hear it in his voice and I could feel a gentle presence emanating from him which had not been there when we first met. (For me, this is the experiential mark of and A to A' shift.) His awareness had grown so that, for him, the realization that he would change the direction of his life and work was quite matter-of-fact.

During the sessions with Earl, my intent had been to be present, to listen and feed back out of a deeper awareness. My principle interest was not his illness, nor in doing something to help the surgery. I was committed to the wholeness we could reach.

The issues that brought him were his; they were the scaffold for our relationship. Nevertheless, I was quite interested to hear what had happened in the surgery and recovery phase. It was only after I began to hear similar reports from others that I appreciated the relationship between wholeness and health.

❋

Life is not a fixed scenario we have to act out. Life is revelation. The whole idea that there is a right way to live is a creation of a very limited part of consciousness. It presumes that we know what is right. We don't. We don't transform by changing what we do; we transform by entering fully into our experience so that we consciously participate in how life is revealing us. The road to avoiding fear or escaping certain experiences is a road of shrinking aliveness. From the perspective of healing it is a dead end. *If we approach our life and healing from the depths of ourselves, any experience has within it the power to transform and heal.*

There is a terrible arrogance in saying that one way is God's and another is not. Any healing must occur from the perspective of the whole, not from the fragmented judgment of human consciousness.

To the usual way of thinking, scientific medicine implies something man-made; therefore it is less "natural" than herbal medicine, energetic medicine (such as acupuncture), or spiritual healing, as in laying on of hands or Reiki. But this understanding is just another splitting game of the basic ego structure. The word *natural* comes from the root *native*, which means "to be born." It is in the experience of living, which is born in the moment, that we express true naturalness. And it is only within this immediacy of living that we can be whole and know ourselves as one with nature. Thus, when we proclaim one thing as natural and something else as not, we are already separate from the immediacy of living. We have forgotten our native being, which is unending emergence, and have moved into a crystalization of separateness. If traditional medicine is "unnatural," then there is no wholeness, and we have "made up" nature and God. They are then just concepts that reside within the ego. But once every experience of life is understood as natural, then we have found a way back to nature and God and our whole selves. And to realize oneself in the wholeness of the moment is literally to be born again.

All ways are God's and are natural, if we could only release our self-created rules and become at-one even for a moment. It is in these moments that the greatest transformations occur. When all the self-conscious involvement falls away and we are unified, it is simply natural to be whole. We can sense that Earl was touching this state in his descriptions of the joy of rolling through the hospital corridor. Clearly, it is as potent to touch such a moment in a hospital elevator as anywhere else. Surgery, a process which we can enter as a true letting-go, can be the door. Understanding this, we realize that all the debate about which treatment is best fills us with so many ways to judge and separate ourselves from our immediate experience that we are fragmented and our energy never reaches full coherence and potential.

When illness arises are we to presume that it is wrong or is our fault? Does the idea that we create our own reality imply that we are the cause of our experiences in the usual way we think of cause—as something that leads to effect? If we say yes, perhaps we may decide that our illness is the result of our lifestyle. In a way, this insight is true, and changes in lifestyle can result in better health. But lifestyle grows not only from the person but also from society and its values. We begin to see that we are not really separate, that our lives are the result of all lives, now and before. Thus we realize that we cannot regard our illness as uniquely caused by ourselves. To say that lifestyle is the cause is a kind of buck passing. Lifestyle is never the cause; it is always already an effect of the consciousness with which we individually and collectively live our lives. If we accept lifestyle as the cause, then every cause is really the effect of a previous cause and on and on until we're back to the Big Bang—and what caused that? This kind of thinking never leads to our own wholeness. But, when we noticed that we were able to modify life by changing lifestyle, it didn't take long before we began prescribing lifestyle changes the way we prescribed other medication!

While it is sometimes true that disease is a reflection of how we live, the mistake is in concluding that how we live is the cause, and then saying, "If I change this or that, I will get well and live better." Such an attitude has grown from applying Newtonian thinking to behavior. We look at effects and then search for causes, thinking this process will tell us about reality. But what this really does is teach us ways to modify personal reality with more concepts. We are no closer to something fundamental. The only thing we can ever really learn from this approach is how to dance with a growing complexity of causes and effects. We can continue to delude ourselves that psychological or physical modifications of our suffering are health. They are not! They just postpone the transformative encounter with ourselves. Modification of illness is not transformation, nor is it ultimately healthy!

Earlier, I stated that the induction sessions with Earl continued until we reached a state of being that felt like love but had no object. We somehow arrived at a state no longer in time. It was something closer to cause, more fundamental. It is hard to describe because each person's experience is unique. But, as I shared with Earl, and later in the group work, certain common features emerged. The sense of being separate from one's experience fell away. Everybody felt a tremendous new sense of their own uniqueness and wholeness, but paradoxically they also felt a commonality with everyone else. When the state was even deeper (and this was much more rare), there was a breakdown of subject/object consciousness and a few individuals entered mystical realization of the Oneness of existence.

All of these experiences represent degrees of attunement to an existing wholeness that is prior to our ordinary awareness. To touch this, even minimally, is to receive the restorative quality of the Whole. But to seek it in order to be healed would be a manipulation of life and an avoidance of what it has to teach us. To the degree that we are unable to sense wholeness, our world is perceived in ever more complex experiences of separation and cause/effect concerns. To the degree that we realize the Prior Wholeness, we are made whole. (If there is one disorder that eclipses all others in this world, it is that our capacity to manipulate reality materially and subtly far exceeds our capacity to recognize life's Wholeness.)

Earl showed me how easy it is to take ideas like "we create our own reality" and draw erroneous conclusions. Earl heard this to mean that he was responsible for the disease rather than for his wholeness. But the statement, "we create our own reality" only has meaning from the space of Wholeness or Oneness, in which the experiencing self is not separate from the experience. As this "I" exists, so exists reality. In this sense "I" creates reality. Only in this state is it true that we are what we think, for thinking is inseparable from being, not something used to manipulate our lives. When we translate this higher state to ordinary consciousness, it becomes distorted into a cause/effect relationship. This is why pseudo-spiritual philosophies that teach us how to use the conscious mind to influence the larger unconscious without honoring Divine Wholeness can be destructive. Using thought in this way (affirmations and visualizations are but two examples) is a kind of violence against Reality as it is, for we are already rejecting our experience and directing our thought to try to make things the way we want. This is a naive attempt to play God! If we want to use the conscious mind to influence the deeper consciousness, we must understand the limitations of conscious awareness and turn the conscious mind towards Prior Wholeness. This is the essence of consecration.

If we look for the cause of our condition in that which we can perceive or explain, we can never find it. The cause is imminent in and inseparable from what we perceive and are. Cause is not anything we have done. To have arrived at Cause is to free us from the usual cause/effect concerns so that we are not always at the effect of every good or bad manifestation of life. There is so much love and aliveness in this state that it invariably is accompanied by health. From my point of view, the question of causation and of personal responsibility for health begins again in each moment. There is limited value in looking to the past to figure out how the problem evolved unless we have fears and concerns that must be examined. However, such concerns are just the starting point of our inquiry, not something to be focused on for themselves. We learn not to inquire after explanations but after aliveness.

Suppose I say, "Yes, I caused this disease through my anxiety about security and money. I always worried whether the kids would have enough and never really looked after myself." This may be true, but from the perspective of healing, we have only taken a step close to wholeness if such inquiry begins to show us the superficiality of such ideas. As we have seen, such an approach never leads to understanding cause, but instead fuels our insatiable self-involvement, which is the very root of our separateness. In fact, it becomes very easy to blame ourselves now that we have a little insight. If we do, the intensity of such feelings create even more self-involvement and separation.

Suppose we forgive ourselves because we see that our upbringing led us to these preoccupations. I have listened to these sorts of explanations again and again. We have found a spurious cause, generated guilt and a sense of failure because of it, and then released ourselves from this self-created tension through "forgiveness." In this kind of psychological masturbation, we never step out of the box of our own separateness. An individual cannot forgive himself, nor anybody else through any action of the conscious mind. True forgiveness is a spontaneous state inseparable from Wholeness. Forgiveness and understanding accompany the sense of Oneness and are Grace. Such Grace is more available to us when we recognize the illusory nature of conscious efforts and turn intuitively and wholeheartedly into the immediacy of our lives. In the moment of unconditional surrender and openness, as we face surgery or any other encounter with the unknown, we become available to a higher level of our being. It seems that we are trapped in a low energy state when we explain our condition with ideas that are themselves part of the limited awareness that is defining the condition in the first place.

Let whatever you're experiencing be the starting point, for example, not understanding the route to wholeness: What does this feel like? Does the feeling localize anywhere in the body? What happens as you just rest with the feeling or simply try to give it words without explaining or judging it?

Usually at this point the feeling changes. The mind begins to block and say, "I don't understand." Irritation, frustration, confusion, anger, helplessness, and tears often result. Don't invalidate what is happening. Do any pictures, associations, memories arise? Let them, without trying to explain them. Just keep relaxing into whatever comes next. Soon you will find the part of yourself that wants to finish the experience trying to get it to make sense. This is the part that keeps saying, "Now I see." But there is a deeper space, and as you approach it you may find yourself beginning not to know what you feel or beginning to feel empty. Just allow it.

Lao Tzu, the Chinese philosopher, said long ago that the great transmuter is acceptance. To accept a feeling is not to agree to it or like it, but to receive it so we are no longer separate from it; we have made it ourselves. And whatever we make an indivisible part of ourselves ceases to have authority over us simply because it is us. At the moment we reach this deeper feeling or awareness that hides just a few layers below the surface, we can merge with it and expand or split away once again into questions and concerns. Now, I don't mean that we have the conscious choice to merge. It is not so easy. Merging can be the conscious consecration, but the actual moment of resolution is a mystery, an act of grace, and it may not happen just because we want it to. But when we have done what we can to bring ourselves to that unity, then we must let go. We don't have to understand ourselves to be at our highest energy states. Usually, the full significance of our illness or the struggle to prepare for the surgery doesn't reveal itself until we actually let go into the experience.

7 * LIFE AS A LOVER

---

*Love alone is capable of uniting living beings in
such a way as to complete and fulfill them, for it
alone takes them and joins them by what is deepest
in themselves.*

TEILHARD DE CHARDIN

DURING THE SUMMER OF 1978 I had a vivid
dream concerning a very close friend of mine, Grace. In the
dream I see her sobbing. She tells me she has a tumor and asks
me to find a doctor for her. I tell her the tumor is not malignant
and she will be all right. I send another woman off to find a surgeon for her. (Grace already has a doctor, but she wants me to
find another.) As she cries, I take her in my arms and tell her I
love her. In the last sequence of the dream, her skin becomes inflamed and seems to peel in places. I hold her in profound love
and she becomes calm, radiant, and happy.

After I finished an intuitive scan of the dream, I was left with a deep longing to tell Grace I loved her. I decided to call her. "Why are you calling me? Certainly not just to tell me you love me?" I mentioned I had had a dream and she asked me about it. I felt reluctant to tell her the whole dream, so I simply said I had seen her in a difficult and painful situation and she had called upon me for help. I told her the dream had evoked so much love for her that I just wanted to call and tell her.

I forgot about the dream until some months later when the phone rang. The voice on the other end said, "Richard, this is your dream. I have a brain tumor."

Diagnostic tests revealed that Grace had a walnut-sized tumor located between the cerebral hemispheres. Her age plus the location and discreteness of the tumor suggested it was probably nonmalignant. However, the surgical process itself would be formidable. Her head would be shaved, the scalp retracted, the top of her skull removed! The tough dura and other membranes covering the brain, which are rich in blood vessels, would have to be cut and pulled back so that the cerebral hemispheres could be parted. At that point the tumor would be dissected out, the blood vessels feeding it tied off.

Until the actual surgery, it would not be possible to know how complicated the removal would be, how much if any normal brain tissue might be disturbed with the possible consequence of permanent neurological damage, or if the tumor was, in fact, nonmalignant.

Her case was an emergency. It was not a question of having many days or weeks or even months in which to contemplate the procedure. The pressure was building in her brain and would kill her. The operation needed to be done as soon as possible.

But the first issue was whether Grace felt trust and rapport with her surgeon, and the second, whether she would have adequate support. The original X-rays and diagnosis had been undertaken by a neurosurgeon near where she lived. She had a background in the health professions and she could recognize the proficiency with which this first surgeon dealt with her. However, while she had no doubts about his competence, she did not feel any connection to him as a human being. Furthermore, she had just moved to a new city, and to undertake such a tremendous process with only her fiance as a support community felt wrong. So she had called me to recommend someone in the vicinity of her former home, which was also near her family and me.

I accompanied her on the visit to the new surgeon. He had been one of my mentors when I was in training, and I respected his professional skill, but also the quality of humanness which he always brought to his work. I felt intuitively that Grace would feel better about this man than she had the first doctor.

It was good to see him again. He did an excellent job of explaining the situation to her. There was no question that a tumor existed, that it was pressing upon the brain giving her double vision and headaches, and that it had to be removed very soon. He took the time to tell her, malignant or not, it was a major surgical process, and carefully explained some of the possible complications, while at the same time reassuring her that he had a great deal of experience and an excellent team. They would do their best.

She was not passive. She asked questions and listened carefully while he answered. What she listened for was the timbre of his voice, the sense of him as a human being. She already felt that I would not have recommended him if he weren't a highly competent physician, but it was important for her to feel that she liked and respected him.

Finally, it was arranged that she be admitted to the hospital that evening, prepared the next day, and operated on the following morning. As we were leaving, I looked at the surgeon and realized how exhausted he was. I asked him in front of "his" patient to get some rest before the operation. His response was wonderful. There was no anger or irritation at having had his own fatigue pointed out to him. Instead, he acknowledged it and said, "I promise that tomorrow night I'll get a massage and be in bed at nine, and when I come to see you in the morning before surgery, I'll be thoroughly rested."

I cannot begin to tell you how important it is that this kind of honesty be shared between the patient and every other person who is involved. It's not merely because it instills confidence in the patient, or a trust in the humanity of the physician. It is equally important that a physician be in touch with his own humanity and capable of being honest about it in front of a patient. Such openness bridges a psychic gulf that separates us because of relative roles. If we live within the boundary of these roles, the flow of love and life force between us is inhibited. But if our role is just our form of service and not a form of exclusive identity, we are joined at the deeper level of our common humanness. This greater connectedness results in a greater energetic potential prior to and during the operation and directly augments the healing potential of that experience.

Must we like our doctor? Or, for that matter, does our doctor have to like us? While we may not immediately like an individual at the personality level, we must have an unqualified sense of appreciation for the person as a human being. This includes a sense of respect and understanding that embraces gifts as well as limitations. When a healer does not have this feeling for the human beings with whom he works, he should retire from work until he can see more compassionately into life. On the patient's side, it is not enough to be in awe of your physician's fame or skill. You must feel a deeper part of yourself has touched him and that he is available to you. However, this doesn't mean that you run around checking out doctors until you find one who is compatible. It means that all of us have to learn more about ourselves! The more whole we are in ourselves, the more people are likeable and the more available we are to each other. In fact, it is my experience that when we know ourselves and are open to life, we are effortlessly drawn to the person who will be an excellent healer for us. The reciprocal situation is also true. As a healer deepens in his own awareness, he begins to attract patients who act as teachers, guiding him to further understanding and refinement of his art.

When the ordinary gulf existing between us falls away, every person seems to be a part of ourselves and everyone becomes appreciated. Not appreciating someone is a signal that one of us is defending psychic territory. If we recognize the territory the other is defending because we have come to understand this area in ourselves and are no longer uncomfortable with it, then his or her distance is not a threat and we can work with such a healer successfully. If you want to find a good doctor, or for that matter a teacher for your transformational process, begin by knowing yourself.

Anything undertaken between individuals who have not tried to bridge basic role and personality gaps is incapable of tapping the fullest potential. In short, if you don't like your physician but "he is the best," you are trusting in only half the truth that leads to healing.

Many physicians hide behind their roles. They think that they must remain aloof because their strength lies in their dispassionate assuredness. It is common belief that to get too involved with patients is dangerous; thus, the emphasis is on clinical knowledge and techniques. But what usually underlies this need to master more and more information and technique is a deepseated sense of inadequacy. Accumulating more information may slightly enhance a healer's abilities, but facing this inadequacy and resolving it with understanding leads to humility and compassion. Developing these traits immeasurably enhances one's capacity as a healer.

The belief that it is dangerous to get too close to one's patients is true on one level, because for most people involvement implies emotional dependency as well as a subtle threat to the specialness that keeps us separate and autonomous. Deep emotional involvement may cause us to identify with the other and there is the potential to activate unfaced fears. Healers are usually not even aware of how distanced they remain from their patients until one or the other opens up. I know one young physician who had an auto accident. Somehow the shock of the accident opened him to his own mortality and the illusion of his self-image. When he returned to work in the hospital, he was unable to withstand the intense emotional forces that had always been present but to which he was just now becoming sensitive. He would cry when he injected medications or as he walked past certain patient's rooms. He felt that, previous to the accident, he had somehow lost track of what was really meaningful in life. He had to retire for a while to learn more about himself, but soon afterwards he began to practice medicine with love.

Whereas some dependency *can* come with involvement, it does not need to be debilitating. Beyond emotional dependency is the energetic rapport that occurs as we recognize our basic relatedness. The road to this capacity is not in abandoning ourselves into emotional identification; rather it comes through self-knowledge that reveals the larger spiritual integrity of life and our place within it. If we have not looked at our own fears and needs very deeply, exposure to the vulnerability and fear of another can cause us to shut down our own aliveness unconsciously. This debilitating stance resides partially in a sense that it is our responsibility to make someone else better. But if we have worked with our own feelings we know that this is not the case. Each person must do this for himself, just as each person must learn to walk. We can offer our skills and all of our aliveness but, ultimately, we each must answer to ourselves.

When a person has mastered his own emotional reactivity, he radiates a presence that allows others not only to experience their own feelings but also to master them. It is the healer's inability to enter the arena of these powerful feelings that causes the patient to suppress his feelings. Since suppressed energy cannot be transmuted to a higher potential, both doctor and patient then enter their healing interaction at a lowered potential.

There is another dimension beyond technique and skill. It is a dimension involved with the quality of our consciousness as we act. And this quality cán imbue our actions with a kind of presence which goes far beyond what skill alone will accomplish. In a sense, it's the age-old observation that there is a difference between a technician and an artist and that the difference is not of this world. He who does not cultivate the radiance of transforming consciousness is poor, indeed.

Grace and her physician liked and respected each other almost immediately, so they were off to the best possible beginning. But now came the really difficult part: for Grace to face the awesomeness of what was unfolding so as to release fully into her experience. This meant she had to face all thoughts and fears concerning what was happening. These were formidable.

She felt that she had betrayed her own spiritual process and thus invited the tumor. For some years, she had made transformation the focus of her life, in large part because of my influence. Then the inner world began to become too overwhelming and her commitment to self-knowledge wavered. Deciding that she was not sufficiently grounded in the world, she had taken a job in industry that had occupied all of her time and energy for the last few years. She had given little thought to her inner process. Furthermore, she came from a religious family and feared having betrayed her spiritual side. She suspected her emphasis on career had resulted in a blocked energy that eventually led to her disease.

The analyst in my consciousness appreciated her insight, partially agreed, and secretly wanted to reward her for it by engaging it even more. But I knew that this kind of understanding has very little value in the process of coming to wholeness. Wholeness is not something we become; it is something we already are, and analysis in itself can never reveal this to us. But a shock such as a brain tumor often can. Grace didn't have much time. It was not a question of whether she had betrayed life, but whether right now, in the immediacy of this hideous nightmare, life had betrayed her.

All the other concerns, questions and feelings were masking

this more fundamental issue. By projecting the sense that she had betrayed herself, she could avoid the immediate problem of her relationship to life right now. Was life a lover or a betrayer?

She realized that she faced a great likelihood, not so much of dying, but of emerging from the operation crippled. In a very short time they would come and cut off her beautiful long hair, her scalp would be peeled back, her skull top removed. She could awaken and discover that it was a malignant tumor and that she had only weeks or months to live. Only in the last year had she been in a fulfilling relationship and marriage was approaching. Now this was all being taken away from her. Was life a lover or a betrayer?

This question is not an intellectual one. When it is asked, it is our whole being that answers. We must not decide that the concept of life as lover is very appealing, and therefore choose that attitude. The fact is, we can choose with our minds, but our being can act as though the moment were betrayal and threat. The position that life is betraying us is usually an unconscious stance, but, if we can recognize it and shift, our entire relationship to existence changes and we become whole in our experience.

The position that life is betraying us, that it is wrathful, stands in a long historical line. Perhaps it is an evolutionary decision. For when we are aligned against life (which is another way of saying that life or God is wrathful), we unwittingly have taken our stand in a level of individuality. "We" are suffering; "we" have lost our connection to God, to truth; "we" are being punished. Therefore, "we" must have done something wrong. The other side of this is that "they" did it; it is "their" fault. "They" can be our parents, the government, the establishment, the job, the elements. If life as it unfolds right now is the betrayer, this is precisely because "me" is predominant. The price we pay is to be cut off from the wholeness and continuity of life, and we cease to be capable of sustaining consciousness of the Divine. Moreover, we have demonstrated to ourselves that we are helpless.

Simultaneously, of course, "we" have to do something. This stance may be intrinsic to our society, to its relationship to the earth, to our attitude toward the other forms of life we share it with. It may well be the basis of our tremendous "conquest" of the environment. For one will conquer a betrayer, but one can never conquer a lover. To conquer a lover is antithetical to love.

But to embrace life, the present moment, with the overwhelming pain and fear intrinsic in Grace's experience is a level of understanding beyond most people. Instead, we remain at a superficial level. We fill ourselves with explanations of how we have arrived where we are, how we have betrayed life, or how we have been manipulated by life or others. We put it in "God's hands." We feel guilty, angry, helpless—so many things, and all of them "natural." I have felt all these things myself many times. But in so doing, "we" remain intact and separate, stuck in our process of reviewing the past, fantasizing about the future, and relating to our own concept of God. We never find out the nature of the love affair that is occurring right now. We are afraid it is not a love affair. This is the fundamental fear. We must pass through this fear in order to enter the next evolutionary understanding.

But the moment we realize that life is a love affair, at that precise moment we know the choices we made in our life were the best at that time. We are no longer the cause of our problems. Life is not punishing us. From the perspective of this realization, nothing in life (no trauma, no injustice) has ever biased us so that wholeness could not be realized. With my awakening experience, I realized all at once that my life existed as a whole—it only appeared to exist in time—and every moment of it was a necessary and inseparable part of the wholeness I now was. Thus nothing was ever wrong. Of course, psychologically much was wrong and people can and will spend tremendous amounts of energy trying to understand this wrongness, just as I did. However, from the perspective of the realization of true wholeness, these efforts just mark time. A tiger pacing in its cage can make all kinds of movements to help discharge some of its energy—and this will make it feel better—but until it is free, it will never be able to access its full energy and know who it really is.

To realize wholeness one must begin from wholeness. This is not possible without first realizing that the essence of life is love. We are in every moment lover and beloved.

And this is how true forgiveness comes about. This is the moment in which we are forgiven our own trespass against life (for to trespass means to encompass less than the whole) and simultaneously, we forgive those who have treated us in such a way that they denied our wholeness. In this moment in which we are whole, we are able to meet our experience and we are reconciled with all that has happened to us.

But the moment of entering this state is itself a mystery. Try to tell someone it is necessary to let go into experience, that it is not the enemy, that right now life is loving him or her through these terrifying moments. At best you can give only a temporary glimpse, a momentary break from pain, for the nature of realization is that it must be experienced firsthand. Thus, all I could do for Grace was love her, just as in the dream. I could suggest that she had made the best choices she could at each point in her life, and that the best choice she could make now was to be as vulnerable to her experience as possible. The experience itself would be the teacher, and if even for a moment the teacher was also a lover, the lesson learned might be the greatest life offers.

The gift of realization does not mean that life will be without pain. It offers a new understanding and a new relationship to life, so that the pain becomes a door which makes life and God a more direct and immediate part of oneself. Still, to stand before another and point him into the immediacy of his experience when it is so overwhelming is something undertaken only in deepest humility. One must live in constant remembrance of one's own ignorance, and the relationship to the sense of life's intrinsic wholeness and love must be real. For if we are urging another toward the abyss of the unknown, we must live at that edge ourselves. Under any appearance of sureness must be the deepest vulnerability to the Divine.

I believe all individuals are protected from the possibility of a major opening in consciousness by a deeper wisdom. Thus I do not ask everyone to have such a realization. For some, to pursue it aggressively would actually be more destructive than enwholing. The energies touched in moments of wholeness shatter our old reality, and we may not find it easy to build a new one unless we have been prepared through a growing inner balance, humility and adoration for life. However, disease creates this kind of situation. It undoes the old life, opens us to new ideas and values, and humbles us. To whatever degree a person who is ill can allow the falling away of his old world and embrace life as it is (that is, act as a lover to the experience), he or she accesses some of the energies of the greater realization. To touch this space even a little seems to make possible a new life, and in some instances, a remarkable regeneration of the body.

This rarely happens, because the very possibility is not recognized. Once the possibility is presented, we must not pursue it like a new drug to get the cure we want. Rather, like a lover, it must be courted with patience. First, we must recognize how natural such a relationship to existence really is; we knew it in the innocence of childhood, but were not conscious of what we knew. Every individual has access to some fundamental religious understandings: a sense of the interconnectedness of all things, the hidden beauty that can surprise us in any moment, the vague feeling of having once known perfect wholeness. These become dormant in the process of developing our individuality, but now they must come forward. Otherwise the stress of facing death and annihilation is too awesome, and we resort to basic psychological defenses such as denial. Or we continue to try to figure it all out and do the right thing, and without knowing it, have diminished our aliveness.

In the case of Grace, she had deep support. I provided some, but more important, there was love within her family that was unusually mature. The values of her family and her own explorations of consciousness represented a substantial foundation for Grace. The day before the surgery, and in the following days, she had a basic wisdom in her relationship to life. She asked deep questions without ultimately having to know the answers. She could simply rest in the moment-to-moment relationship to life.

The kind of inquiry she made during that day prior to the surgery—her ruthless examination of values and motives, what had been important in her life and the direction in her life—was an act of profound courage. But most important was her relationship to her immediate feelings. She cried a great deal, kept letting go, would laugh and then cry some more. The process was one of trying to find the symphony in a cacaphony of feeling. When she attempted to explain herself or to figure out anything, I just waited silently. At other moments she would speak of the paradox and confusion, and then briefly realize that in some sense this was really no different than any other moment. When I spoke, it was only to join her in what felt immediate and direct.

I could feel a strength emerging. It was not that she was strong in the sense of control. Rather, her strength resided in her openness to wave after wave of undisguised feeling. I made no effort to have her control any of this. I did not really know what I would do in her situation. However, as I allowed myself to resonate and call forth to the underlying fullness that was building, a presence began to fill the room and we became silent. It was a silence shot through with a sense of connectedness although I wouldn't say we were connected to each other. Rather, we were connected to something else, a sense of divine ignorance, a living emptiness.

This territory is a place where an individual makes peace with himself and his creator. It is not a place of words and thought; it is a dimension beyond thought. Out of the feeling of this space, Grace arranged to have Communion services on the morning before the surgery. Her father performed the ceremony. The surgeon, the anaesthetist, myself, and her family members all attended. At the conclusion of the ritual, several of us entered into that inner state of quiet and rapport that allowed energy sharing. I had shared this with her the day before as well. This time we directed the energy flow not only to her, but also to the surgeon. (See Door 5, The Energy Embrace.)

She was taken to the operating room, as opened and surrendered as she could be, and underwent a ten-hour surgical procedure. We all remained in meditation and contemplation for a portion of that time. The news that it was a nonmalignant tumor brought joy to all of us. When we heard it had been removed completely, a great sigh of relief went through the family.

But the real evidence of the depth of her preparation came later. When the surgeon emerged, he reported that he had just operated for ten-and-a-half hours, but he felt more energized than he had when he started. He said he often felt good after a long surgery, especially a successful one, although he would feel fatigue. But in this instance, he felt tremendously rejuvenated. There were times, he said, when he felt our presence in the room with him.

But he was most excited because the operation itself was quite miraculous. He said although he had typed and cross-matched her blood for a minimum of four units, and was prepared to call for more, after ten-and-a-half hours of major surgery no transfusion was necessary. In fact, he estimated she had lost in total perhaps a half unit of blood. This was extraordinary!(7)

After surgery when he went to examine her in the surgical recovery room, she was already far more conscious than most patients. While he expected to discover some residual nerve loss, he was amazed how tremendously improved she was. All the problems that had existed while the tumor was in place were gone. In fact, her general alertness was returning much faster than is common for patients who have undergone such an immense procedure. And, while she was in pain, there was no question that she was in an uncanny state of recovery. The case was so unusual that he intended to write it up for the medical journals.

Her recovery continued to be quite outstanding. She was walking within a few days and, while she had pain, responded to medication so well that she was able to use smaller and smaller doses. She was discharged from the hospital in six days, which is an unusually rapid recovery from such a procedure.

Her convalescence after that was uneventful until one night she phoned me in tears. Her skin was inflamed and in places it was peeling. This turned out to be a reaction to one of the medications she was taking. It was my dream again, and I had to laugh. She had managed to face the tremendous experience of her surgery, but on her way to recovery she couldn't find a relationship to itchy skin. When I reminded her to stop fighting and explore new relationships to the sensations and to her fear of missing sleep, she immediately centered and the itching became easily tolerable. Once the medication was changed, the problem ceased. Today she leads a life of full health.

Here again was confirmation that the consciousness with which we enter a process such as surgery, and the depth of rapport we allow with each moment, with our family and friends, and with our health care team, can augment healing. Of course, there is no way to measure the transformative impact of such an event.

This experience showed me how essential the relationship between the patient and physician is to maximizing the healing potential of any medical event. There was something inspiring about the way the physician agreed to prepare himself and the spontaneous unfolding that brought us all together for the ritual prior to surgery. This experience could happen everywhere. There is no magic secret. All we have to do is be more honest with ourselves and a little more available to the energetic presence that is ever awaiting.

❀

And what about my dream? Yes, there was an unusual accuracy in it. Did this prophetic dream in some way foreshadow the remarkable nature of this experience and perhaps help bring it about? I cannot say. As Grace's experience unfolded, closely mirroring the dream, the certainty of her eventual well-being, as foretold by the dream, provided a contrast to the probability of disaster suggested by the situation. My medical mind looked at one reality while another part of me simply was present with no sense of concern.

Part III

Doors to
Greater Aliveness

1 ✿ STREAM-OF-CONSCIOUSNESS WRITING

THIS IS A WRITING EXERCISE, and I recommend a spiral notebook and a ballpoint pen. A pen is preferable to a pencil because you won't be interrupted to sharpen the point.

Begin by sitting in a comfortable writing position. Set a timer or leave a clock in easy view. To start, write for thirty minutes at a time.

Begin to write a simple description of anything you are feeling or sensing. *Sensing* here refers to any sensation (for example, the sensation of the pen in your hand, the pressure of your bottom against the seat, any places where you sense pressure, weight, heat or cold). Sensing also includes what you are seeing, hearing, smelling and tasting. In other words, begin to write down whatever you *notice*—whatever is reported to your awareness through any of the senses.

Don't censor what you write. If it comes into your awareness, write it. However, there is no need to write the whole sensation. Thus, if you are feeling the edge of the desk under your forearm, you don't have to write "edge of desk under my forearm." Just write "pressure, forearm." You might notice the pressure has more characteristics. If it feels warm, write "warm." Don't pause to evaluate what you are sensing. Just move randomly from one perception to another. There is no need to explain any of them or to try to describe in great detail. The key is to write continually, recording however you wish, the immediate sensations and perceptions entering your awareness. You will notice that you are perceiving more than you can write. Don't be concerned. Just write as quickly as you can, moving from one perception to the next. Here is an example: "Fingers curled, typewriter, wind, shadow moving, weight on buttocks, seat back, shoulders tight, jaw clenched, eyes softening, itchy nose, sound of typewriter, warmth in belly, mouth dry, dog barking, hesitation . . . ."

As you are writing, you'll notice other aspects of awareness, such as thoughts and feelings. Report these also, as briefly as possible. There is one crucial attitude: *Don't explain the thoughts or the feelings.* Rather than recording the thought, write "thinking." If there is a feeling, report it. For example, if suddenly you feel afraid, write "afraid." But don't explain it. Don't write "afraid because tomorrow is the surgery." Instead, stay present with what is coming into your awareness. Write "thinking, sad, fear, back hurts, tongue on teeth, eyebrow itches, thinking, worry, sad, hesitation, confusion, flower vase, toes curled, lick lips, sigh, deep breath, light pain in shin, pressure side of foot, thinking, fear, tired, thinking" and so on.

The important point is *not to analyze.* This exercise is designed to notice the flow of awareness but not interfere with it. It is absolutely essential that you just keep writing and get away from the tendency to analyze, interpret, or explain anything.

When we interpret a feeling, particularly a complex emotion, we rarely interpret it correctly. True, we explain it so that we think we understand why we are feeling it. But this is just an illusion. The thoughts about an emotion never explain the emotion, they just substantiate it. Likewise, emotions generate thoughts, but these thoughts only serve to substantiate the emotion or avoid it. They never explain it. For example, if you are angry and believe it is because so and so did such and such, you are incorrect. The anger and the thought are part of a single configuration. Separate one from the other and soon the anger is gone. Thus a deeper explanation of anger implies moving to a larger dimension. This dimension transcends and therefore includes emotion and thought. From this higher perspective, anger shows an interaction of energies; it is our own rigid perspective that is responsible, not what someone else did.

This exercise begins the process of interrupting what I call the "belly-mind," the mind that grows through the unconscious link-up of thought and emotion. Until this link-up can be suspended, there is very little chance of centering in a deeper space, because the emotions that surround a health crisis (or any personal crisis) are usually very potent.

Do this exercise for thirty minutes. When you are finished, stop writing and just notice whatever you are sensing. Is the mind quiet? Is it active? Are you alert, drowsy? Do things look the same? Is there any alteration in the quality of awareness?

Just notice. Don't judge. There is no goal in this exercise. It allows awareness to open up and become freer. It helps us to expand into our awareness, to become more aware of our bodies, and to notice that thought is just an aspect of awareness and not the whole or even the most important part.

After sitting quietly for two or three minutes (or longer if that feels right for you) get up and go for a walk. Walk as briskly as you can for about twenty minutes and return to the notebook. Set the timer and begin the stream-of-consciousness writing again for thirty minutes. When thirty minutes are up, go out again for a walk. This concludes one round of the exercise.

❀

In the beginning, do this exercise twice a day. But, if you want to intensify your relationship to the immediate present and give your mind and emotions a deeper rest, this exercise can be done for two sittings in the morning and two sittings later in the day.

Don't modify the exercise and indulge writing about any particular thoughts. When you sit to do the stream-of-consciousness writing, just note "thinking" whenever you become aware of getting caught up in an idea or a fantasy, *no matter how important the idea seems*. Going for a walk is an important part of each round. If you are unable to walk, then do the writing and utilize one of the variations suggested below.

Variations

The basic writing process remains the same. However, the contrast of other dynamics can involve working in the garden for awhile or jogging for ten or fifteen minutes rather than walking. If physical activity is not possible, then listen to a piece of music. Choose music that tends to evoke a deeper space. (See suggestions at the end of Door 2.) Another alternative to physical activity is to meditate, hum, or sing.

Commentary

Read this section after having explored the exercise several times.

The value of this exercise is that it suspends time. Ordinarily, we are caught up in past or future. We have things to do that concern us or things we are anticipating. When we are approaching something like surgery, or when an illness has interrupted the usual flow of our lives, it does not interrupt the flow of thought. Thus we can spend a great deal of time dwelling in feelings and thoughts. All emotions evoke thought and many thoughts tend to evoke emotion. The circle of thought and emotion is a closed circuit. It closes out other kinds of awareness, such as simply being present.

Since the process of thinking invariably involves the future or the past, our overall energy level (bodily and psychic) tends to be dispersed and lowered. The greatest energy occurs when we are fully present in the moment and have lost self-conscious preoccupation. By exploring stream-of-consciousness writing, we are drawn into the present and our energy heightens. At a higher energy we are no longer as vulnerable to the thoughts and feelings that dominate us when we are at a lower energy. We gain authority over our own space. The mind and emotions begin to calm. This can be very important in healing, because we need all of our energy.

I remember the first time I explored this exercise. I had broken up with my girlfriend just as I completed my internship. I was about to start a private medical practice, but all I could think about was my sense of emptiness, anxiety and loneliness. I kept fantasizing about how we could get back together, and I was terrified that suddenly my sense of purpose had disappeared. It was all I could do to shop for food and cook a meal for myself. I called a meditation teacher and asked for help. He suggested the stream-of-consciousness writing.

I set aside a weekend and set up a schedule whereby I wrote for thirty minutes, sat in meditation for thirty minutes, and then went for a walk. I made sure I had plenty of juice and fruit around so that I wouldn't have to concern myself about shopping or preparing meals. I repeated the process all through the day until night. Then I showered and went to sleep. I noticed, during the gaps preceding each round of writing, that I was no longer anxious, and even doing the dishes began to have an appeal. The next day I repeated the process. By that evening I was in an entirely clear state of consciousness. I felt as though I had awakened from a dream, that all my pain was due somehow to having lost my sense of self. When we separated, a large part of me went with her. But by becoming present to myself in the moment I was restored. Of course, the pain came back at times, but never with that near-paralyzing sense of loneliness and anxiety.

This episode taught me that we cannot know our full capacity when we are disconnected from ourselves. When our energy is divided and lowered, we are at the mercy of our fears. No amount of self-analysis or talking (I was in therapy at the time) can begin to unify one's being as deeply as just committing into the moment. By using a method such as the stream-of-consciousness writing, a person can become centered. The dissipation of energy that comes with the knot in the belly-mind can be untied. In this more centered and unified state of awareness we have much greater capacity to meet a challenging situation.

Once again we are reminded that our strongest condition is one of unity within. To find unity we must enter a dimension that transcends thought and emotion. This dimension is one of energy or presence that is available to all of us when we are centered in ourselves and fully present. Now.

DOOR

2 * LISTENING TO MUSIC

All music is what awakes from you when you are
   reminded by the instruments
It is not the violins and the cornets—it is not the
   oboe nor the beating drums, nor the score of the
   baritone singer singing his sweet romanca—nor
   that of the women's chorus,
It is nearer and farther than they.

                    WALT WHITMAN

THE USE OF MUSIC to induce deep relaxa-
tion and altered states of consciousness has been an important
aspect of my work. It is a way simultaneously to bring a whole
group to an identical energy, and this results in an intensified
presence that accelerates individual opening. Some years ago, I
was invited to bring my work to a Tibetan meditation center.
At the end of the five-day conference, some of the monks

remarked that the music process was the fastest tool they knew for creating expanded awareness. They had been using chanting and meditation techniques that were the products of an ancient tradition. With the easy availability of fine-quality, inexpensive stereo equipment, anyone who is not exploring the fantastic wealth of music is missing one of the most important gifts of modern technology to humanity.

All music carries an aliveness that reflects both the composer's and performer's state of consciousness. In certain pieces the effect upon a relaxed and open listener can be quite profound. The music can activate energy centers, free areas of repressed energy, induce spontaneous reverie and imagery, and, in general, create a space to let go of control and expand boundaries. The key to the potential of the music is, first, the state of consciousness of the listener and, second, the quality of energy inherent in the music itself. Thus listening to music becomes a mirror of our own openness, as well as a way of learning to surrender more deeply. However, I have observed that many of us really don't know how to listen. We listen with our heads, with our critical faculties, comparing this music to that music, or comparing our experience of the music to former experiences with the same or other music. What I want to describe here is listening to music from the heart and with the whole body.

In my work, I play the music very loudly so that the whole body is vibrated and resonated. However, this is something one cannot ordinarily do and it is not necessary for our purposes. The important thing is to let go into the music, to become lost in it. In order to do this, you begin by giving yourself permission to get lost. Lie down on the floor or in bed. Lie on your back rather than your stomach to keep from falling asleep. Also, the supine position tends to encourage openness and expansiveness.

Choose a piece of music intuitively by going to your music collection, closing your eyes and handling one record or tape after another. As soon as you feel a sense of connectedness, choose that one. If you find it is a piece you don't particularly care for, **try** it anyway. After all, we want to explore having a new relationship to the music. Even music we don't ordinarily like, if listened to from the heart – that is, without a sense of separation – can have a completely new significance. (At the end of the chapter is a list of music I recommend. These selections are pieces I have used over the years. Some generate an expansive or uplifting effect, while others can be quite emotionally provocative. Explore these pieces on your own and discover your relationship to them.)

Another way to choose a piece of music is to feel into your mood and see if any piece of music comes to mind. Sometimes I notice before a conference session that I am spontaneously humming a particular piece or hearing it in my mind; I will play that piece during the session if I can recognize it. There are many ways to choose, but try not to get too analytical about it. Trust a first impression. It doesn't really matter if the music is just right. What is more important is whether you can let go into it.

Obviously, some music is more difficult to relax into. However, I have learned that we can listen to music that is unfamiliar and even uninteresting or unpleasant to one part of us, but as we let go deeper, a larger part of us is able to merge into the music. If you find yourself critically noticing the quality of the recording or you own response to it, relax this part of yourself, for it is not the whole of you. In fact, in this context, such a stance is a defense against letting go. It is by letting go of first one relationship and then another to the experience of listening that you are carried into a deeper space. Imagine a cloud vaporizing off dry ice. Let critical thoughts gently evaporate like the dry ice. If you find it hard to let go, do not contract away from the immediate moment. Just notice that it is difficult. Relax, drift outward, and be carried away by the music. This will become much clearer as you actually begin to explore the music.

One final suggestion: Before starting the piece and during the first few minutes, allow your breathing to become regular. Focus your awareness in the center of your chest so that it feels as though you are breathing in and out through the chest. As you do this, you may notice some kind of sensation building. It may feel like warmth or it may become a pressure. It is also fine if there is no sensation. If any physical sensation occurs, let that diffuse throughout your body by relaxing your awareness of it so that the feeling can evaporate outward like the dry ice. When breathing into any energy center, above all, do not force. If a tightening sensation should develop, become more relaxed as you breathe out and let your attention diffuse to the whole body rather than focusing on just one area. Imagine that your whole body is porous and translucent, so that the sensation disperses because there is nothing containing it.

Once you have allowed this awareness for a few minutes, join your breathing to the music as though you were breathing the music in and out of you. Don't inhale it into your lungs. Let your whole being breathe the music. As you breathe in, become receptive to the music. It is a receptiveness that is unconditional. In a sense, this kind of receptiveness doesn't really know that it is music. It would be more accurate to say that as you breathe in, you become receptive to whatever is happening within and around you. As you breathe out, surrender utterly, allowing yourself to dissolve into the music and into the whole of your experience. At a certain point, you may just get lost in the music, and that is best of all. When you do come back into more ordinary awareness, accept it utterly and let your awareness of being back in self-consciousness relax away just like the dry ice vaporizing into space. Keep letting go in this way until the music is over.

Hand Positionings

On some occasions you may want to listen to music with your hands positioned over your body. This allows the flow of bodily energies to be somewhat focused through the hands and can be helpful in alleviating anxiety (see position number 2) and restlessness (see position number 3). Certain states of consciousness that can be deeply enwholing are associated with anatomical areas. In my experience, the heart or mid-chest is associated with the awakening of the deeper current of energy and the first sense of unconditional love. The activated lower abdomen resolves the fear of annihilation and creates a special kind of relationship to the physical environment. It is a state much prized by practitioners of martial arts. Placing the hands doesn't necessarily mean that these areas will become activated; however, a subtle alteration of consciousness does occur. Please don't get involved in any esoteric concerns; just place your hands if you feel like experimenting.

In some positions you may need to use a few pillows or a folded towel to support your arms comfortably.

Position 1: Let your palms rest over your mid-chest and heart.

Position 2: Place one palm over the solar plexus (the upper part of the abdomen just below the breast bone). Place the other palm over the mid-chest. Explore on your own to see if there is any difference when the hands are reversed.

Position 3: Place one palm over the lower abdomen and the other palm behind the neck and base of the skull. This may not be comfortable for very long. When it becomes uncomfortable, move to a comfortable position.

The most important thing is not the placement of hands. It is far more important to let go into the music than to be concerned with the hands. I suggest the hand positions because they tend to redirect bodily energies (which may open up and heighten during the music) back into the body and psychic centers. I know that to touch oneself tenderly while letting go into music or just letting go into the moment can have a beneficial effect. When I was traveling throughout the world and had eaten strange food, I often would retire to my room and place my hands gently over my abdomen. Then, just as though I were letting go into a piece of music, I would drift into reverie. Since I was already aware of how to activate hand energies, this space was very natural to me. (See Door 5, The Energy Embrace.) I found that even though I traveled in some very exotic and unfamiliar areas, I never developed indigestion.

The energy of the hands, when activated, can also be positioned to ease pain. In a state of quiet, after listening to the music, place your hands over any area that is injured or where there is pain. Just continue breathing gently. As you breathe out, sense your breath flowing out through your hands. Don't try to heal; just be open and receptive to the intrinsic wholeness of life and trust whatever wants to happen.

Commentary

Listening to music, or perhaps it is better to call it dissolving into music, is a very simple but highly valuable tool for bringing ourselves to a sense of ease and inner unity. When our whole attention is absorbed in the music, a degree of unity is reached. And because there is no specific focus, because we are not concentrated as we might be, in something like our work, it is a different kind of unity, a unity that can allow new possibilities. Without doing anything in particular, it is a way to allow our energy body to make its own adjustments and retuning. It does this with its own wisdom when we are highly involved with an experience (surrendered into the wholeness of life) so that our self-conscious apparatus has gotten out of the way. Reaching a deeper unity of consciousness and a greater aliveness cannot be achieved through problem-solving. It is too restricting. Thus to solve this problem we want to explore dis-solving.

We are not aiming for any particular kind of experience. The tremendous value that comes from listening/dissolving is that the music becomes a door into a world different from one's personal inner world. By releasing into music and continuing to let go into it, we create space within consciousness. Often we use our awareness within a fairly specific focus. We aren't even aware of this. It isn't until we let go into a contrasting state that we begin to operate in a new kind of awareness. Consciousness loves contrast!

In order for us to be aware of something, there must be contrast with something else. If we are always in the noise of the city, we don't "hear" the noise until we sit up on the crest of a mountain and marvel at the quiet. If we have been under stress, we will not recognize it until we begin to let go during vacation. These are outer examples, but "consciousness loves contrast" suggests that the very way in which we are aware of ourselves cannot be appreciated until we become aware of ourselves in a different way. Frequently, people are so involved with trying to get well that the parts of themselves that were always waiting to bring them to wholeness are completely missed. Sometimes just surrendering into something as impractical as music brings these parts forward.

Surrendering is not passive. It is not watching television. Television is appealing because it takes us out of ourselves. Its power is in the contrast it provides, for it makes us feel that we are living real experiences, while in fact we are hardly tapping our own aliveness. If television were more consciously created and utilized, it could induct a higher energy and be very healing. Furthermore, even though we are generally unaware of it, millions of people are simultaneously receiving the same input, and there is the possibility of creating a unified and heightened energy field in them even though they are in different places. But as it is, television is mostly a form of escape. When we give ourselves over to television, we give ourselves over to consensus consciousness of the most mediocre level and quality. Thus it only rarely imparts a higher energy.

The word *surrender* means to render to a higher source. When we let go and dissolve into the music, we are surrendering to a higher relationship to life. Surrendering into the music is possible because as we let go of one level of participation we enter the next level, and so on, until we reach a state in which the sense of self as a separate observer has fallen away. The mind is unified—there is no music, there is no listener. This is the point at which a deeper process can work through us. We enter into the experiment of listening/dissolving to allow a natural wholeness to manifest. It is very important that we allow to happen whatever wants to happen. Few people are wise enough to recognize the enwholing nature of certain experiences. We only know how to recognize our idea of what is enwholing.

When a person decides he is willing to explore the multidimensional nature of awareness, it becomes very important to invite several contrasting states of consciousness during the course of a day. This is particularly true when working with illness. The tendency is to hear only the medical perspective, or to consider only the practical concerns, or the sometimes overwhelming emotional dynamics. We end up unwittingly limiting what we will let ourselves explore by taking the easiest and most familiar route. The familiar includes focusing on practical concerns, worrying about what to do, trying to make decisions, organizing oneself, and on and on. It can even include our need to do our special healing meditations and rituals. In fact, this level seems so vital that we hardly realize that other states can bring things together with even more room for higher energy and vitality. Frequently the state most familiar to us is also one in which the energy available is carefully regulated and controlled. For example, George Bernard Shaw used to remark that his most creative moments came spontaneously after he had let go of all his efforts and set aside his work. Then, quite unbidden, a whole new burst of creativity and understanding would carry him into a fresh new perspective. This is precisely what is needed when you are preparing for surgery and want to access the fullest energy for healing.

The fullest energy for healing is not available to us through conscious efforts alone. That is why it is important to allow space for other kinds of awareness. One way this can be accomplished is by listening to music and letting go into it. While our intent may be to grow in awareness, to heal, or even to relax, the actual process of listening/dissolving has its greatest value when we trust whatever it brings and don't try to direct or control it. Quite beyond any particular effort, the very act of becoming absorbed in the music unifies us; we are briefly at-one in our experience. The effect can be tremendously rejuvenating, and it is quite possible to gain new insight simply because for a little while ordinary preoccupations are released.

During a listening session at a conference, one woman suddenly found herself being overwhelmed by a terrible darkness. She was about to scream out when she heard a voice say, "I love you," and without thinking she received the darkness into herself and it became the greatest sense of peace and bliss she had ever known. Her whole body was enlivened in this feeling and it went far beyond anything that ever accompanied her guided meditations or premeditated visualizations. After this, she had a certainty that everything was going to be all right. Some weeks later, as she was going under anaesthesia, she felt the overwhelming darkness again, and this time she consciously said, "I love you." It was her last conscious memory until she awoke after the surgery. The surgery went very well and she recovered rapidly. But, most important, she *knew* that she was healed. It wasn't a thought or an idea or a hope. From that day on she never gave it another thought, and she remains well.

MUSIC LIST

M = Movement
R = Relaxation/Meditation
I = Inspiration

I Bach, 6 *Brandenburgische Konzerte*, K. Richter-Munchener Bach Orchestra Archiv 2708031

I Bach and Handel, Passion Music Kathleen Ferrier Decca KCSP 588

I Beethoven, Symphony No. 5 C. Kleiber Vienna Philharmonic Deutsch gram. 2530 516

I Beethoven, Symphony No. 9 G. Solti-Chicago Symphony London CSP-8

I Beethoven, Violin Concerto in D Isaac Stern/Bernstein Columbia MS6093

M Bolling, Claude, Suite for Flute and Jazz Piano, Rampal Columbia, M33233

I Brahms, Symphony No. 1 (Symphony Nos. 2, 3, 4 also) Bernard Haitink Concertgebouw Orchestra, Amsterdam Phillips 6500 519

I Bruckner, Ninth Symphony Herbert von Karajan, Berlin Philharmonic Deutsch gram. 923078

I   Copland, Aaron, Appalatian
Spring
L. Bernstein
Columbia MG 300 71

M   Dharmama and Meditation
Between
Spectrum SM 1011

I   Debussy, *La Mer*
Deutsch gram. 138923

I, M   Denver, John, It's About Time
RCA AFKI 46833

R   Deuter, George Chatawya
Celebration
Kuckuck 040

R   Deuter, George Chatawya
Ecstacy
Kuckuck LC 2099

R   Dexter, Ron
Golden Voyage
Awakening Productions,
4132 Tullin Ave.
Culver City, CA 90230

I   Dvorak, New World Symphony
Bernstein
New York Philharmonic
Columbia M 31809

I   Fauré, *Messe de Requiem -
Cantique de Jean Racine*
G. Guest, The Choir of St.
John's College, et al.
Argo ZRG 841

M   Flashdance
Polygram Records
811-492-4M1

I   Glass, Philip
Glassworks
CBS 37265

R   Halpern, Steven
Starborn Suite
SRI A80-C

R   Hamel, Peter Michael
NADA
Celestial Harmonies CEL 001

I   Handel, Messiah
Klemperer, Philharmonic
Chorus
Angel CL 3657

I   Harris, Richard
The Prophet
Atlantic SD 18120

I   Harris, Richard
Jonathan Livingston Seagull
Dunhill DSD 50160

I   Hovhaness, Mysterious
Mountain
Chicago Symphony Orchestra
RCS LSC 2251

R, M   Jarre, Jean Michel
Oxygene
Polydor PD-1-6112

R, M   Jarre, Jean Michel
Equinoxe
Polydor PD-1-6175

I   Jarrett, Keith
The Koln Concert
Polydor ECM 1064/65

R   Kelly, Georgia
Seapeace
Box 954, Topanga, CA 90290

R, I   Kelly, Georgia
The Sound of Spirit
Heru 104

R	Kitaro Silk Road Canyon 2LB 051/052	I	Rimski-Korsakov Scheherezade Phillips 7300 226
M,R,I	Mannheim Steamroller Fresh Aire, I, II, III, IV, V Am. gram. AG370	I	Saint Saen: Organ Symphony No. 3 Chicago Symphony Deutsche gram. 2530619
I	Mahler, Symphony No. 1 Bernard Haitink Philips SAL 6500342	I	R. Schumann Symphony No. 4 Deutsche gram. 2530 660
I	Mahler Symphony No. 2 Bernstein Col. M2 32681	I	Smetena, The Moldau Brenstein, New York Philharmonic Columbia M31817
M, I	The Moody Blues Days of Future Past MFSL C-042	I	Star Wars and Close Encounters of the Third Kind Z. Mehta, L.A. Philharmonic London MFSL 1-008
M, I	The Moody Blues A Question of Balance Threshold THS 3		
M, I	The Moody Blues In Search of the Lost Chord DES 18017	R	Sterns, Michael Planetary Unfolding BMI CM1004
M, I	The Pachelbel Canon and Two Suites for Strings Paillard Chamber Orchestra RCA Red Seal FRL 1-5468	I	Tchaikovsky, Swan Lake Ballet Suite and Sleeping Beauty Ballet Suite E. Ormandy, Philadelphia Orchestra Co. M 31838
I, M	Ravel Bolero Deutsch gram. 3335 436-1	I	Tchaikovsky, Symphony No. 5 E. Ormandy, Philadelphia Orchestra Col. M 31842
I	Ravel Daphnis and Cloe Deutsch gram. 138923	I	Tchaikovsky Symphony No. 6 Haitink-Concertgebouw Orchestra Phillips 7300-063
I	Respighi Pines of Rome Deutsch gram. 2530 890-1		

R   Vangelis
Apocalypse des Animaux
Polydor 2489-113

I   Vangelis
Chariots of Fire
Polydor PD 1-6335

M   Vangelis
China
Polydor PD 1 6199

R   Vangelis
La Fête Sauvage
LPL 1-5110 C006-14276

M,I,R Vangelis
Heaven and Hell
RCA/EMI

I   Vaughan Williams, Symphony
No. 6, The Lark Ascending
Sir Adrian Boult, New York
Philharmonic
Angel S-36902

3. HUMMING MEDITATION

BEGIN THIS MEDITATION by getting into a comfortable sitting position. It is helpful not to have any restriction or pressure from clothing. Humming, of course, means a droning sound made with the lips closed. Close your eyes and begin gently humming.

The coordination of the breath with the humming is important, but it is better to discover how to do it on your own. Here are a few suggestions: As you hum, let the breath fall from you, rather than forcing the sound or trying to continue it for a long period. When the relaxed exhalation no longer has the strength to support humming, let the exhalation finish naturally. Then breathe in and allow the hum to happen once again. It is best to let the sound do what it wants. Usually, if you begin to carry a tune or deliberately change the pitch, it indicates self-conscious observation and interaction with the sound. In my experience, the sound changes on its own. Don't focus exclusively on the sound. Instead, let the humming become a vehicle for exploring your whole being, and particularly the relaxation and freedom of your breathing. Finally, as you exhale let the sound sink into the lower belly, and if there is any tension or holding there allow it to become relaxed. You will find that from time to time a new level of relaxation is discovered and the belly becomes softer and softer.

Explore this meditation on your own several times before reading the Commentary. I suggest that humming be explored, at first, for twenty minutes, two or three times a day, staying with it until there is a profound sense of relaxation in the chest and particularly the abdomen.

Commentary

The humming vibration has the capacity to cause a deep-level relaxation. As vibration, humming is a form of consciousness — and therefore a form of information. By vibrating the physical body, it is possible to allow new organization within the muscular and autonomic dynamics which are not ordinarily considered within conscious reach. There is no need to try for any particular response. The rebalancing occurs of itself.

Just as with listening to music, the humming becomes a space where you learn to let go more and more deeply. As you notice yourself thinking about what you are doing, let this awareness go. Gradually the process will generate an altered state of consciousness. This has the value of being a contrast to our ordinary conscious state and thus allowing rebalancing of awareness in ways that go beyond conscious understanding.

Humming into the belly allows a gradual relaxation of the abdomen, while the act of humming is resonating the chest. This facilitates an energetic connection between the chest and abdomen. In my experience, this connection is more important to physical rejuvenation than humming, for example, into the forehead. However, while humming can have a helpful effect upon well-being and is, perhaps, the fastest way that I know of to release anxiety, it is also a way to gather energy and thereby open to new awareness. A case in point occurred one day when I was on an airplane with a friend. There was some turbulence and I could see that he was anxious. He said that flying always made him tense. I suggested that he hum gently and touched his abdomen just below the belly button. "Imagine that you are humming into your lower belly," I told him. He did this for a few minutes and was astonished at the state of calm that emerged. The rest of the flight was clearly a pleasure for him.

As you hum, it is better just to allow it to lead you rather than you leading it in any way. It is valuable to explore humming into other parts of the body and humming into areas of tightness, injury, or pain. When the humming becomes deeply relaxed and the mind has become still, the quality of the humming begins to permeate the whole body. If we can hum in this completely unpremeditated and relaxed way, into any part of the body, it will help rejuvenate that area and awaken the life force therein.

Bodily Feedback Dynamics

The humming is a crucial process because it can lead to a point of unusual relaxation in a particular area of the body. If you have explored humming into various parts of the body, you may have noticed which areas tend to be tense or armored. By exploring humming, you can work to relax these areas in progressively deeper ways.

Very few people are consciously aware that a part of the body can be used as a feedback mechanism to report when aliveness has become contracted. You may not be able to tell directly through self-observation whether your consciousness is more or less open because you are caught up in that awareness. But the body, particularly an area that tends to become tense, can show you.

This understanding can help us learn when we are in new territory for which our usual awareness is not adequate. During a conference we often work with heightened states of consciousness. Frequently, while in a heightened state, people experience such an incredible release of bodily tension and control that after a few days they feel healthier and more rejuvenated than ever before. Such an experience shows that exercise is only a part of staying fit and healthy; an even more important aspect is the level of energy or the quality of consciousness that animates us. However, these heightened states are also new, and often when we are caught up in them we don't realize how we got there. Thus it becomes really important to develop certain postures or body awarenesses as markers or symbols to guide us back to the heightened state. In many ancient religions, certain hand and finger positions are an integral part of religious practice. These remind the worshipper of past states of heightened energy and offer a path through the body to a particular kind of consciousness.

Not everyone can feel the energy directly and move themselves back into an altered consciousness. A first step is to begin to associate a particular quality of consciousness or state of relaxation with the subjective feeling of some part of your body. This is one aspect of how the humming meditation can be applied. For example, the belly is an excellent feedback device for even the most minute shift of energy and awareness. After humming until the belly becomes very soft and feels open, just notice how it feels compared to when you are anxious, hurried, or impatient. By tuning in to the muscular quality of the belly, you can immediately see whether you have become disconnected from a larger consciousness (and at the same time, somewhat disconnected from your body). By breathing or humming a few times into the belly and reproducing the relaxed and flaccid feeling, a sense of letting go and a return to calmness will likely result. If you are sensitive to energy, you will feel the bodily energies and enhancing of radiance around the body.

I have used this approach with a number of people with major disease when they were caught in their heads with ideas about themselves, their spouses, their doctors. These ideas seemed very real and important to them, and undoubtedly they were, but a decreased state of aliveness was one result of them. The work was to release this ordinary level of awareness so that other areas perhaps more radiant with energy could be found. At certain moments, I could sense when this opening occurred, but the minute I tried to point it out to them in words, their minds would click in and the energy would be gone. Finally, I began to watch their bodies intuitively. I could see that as their energy opened up, certain areas of the body became relaxed. I began to have them hold that area very lightly with their hands and, as they spoke, to notice how their bodies were responding.

You can do the same thing with the voice, sensing its resonance as feedback to the depth and wholeness of the state from which a person is speaking. However, this takes practice, and it is often quite difficult for someone to listen to his own voice quality. It is not so difficult to become aware of the belly (or in some cases the jaw, the tongue, or the eyes).

One woman came to see me with her husband. She had cancer, and felt that part of it was due to problems in the marriage. She felt that her husband was not loving enough and did not know how to honor what, to her, was very important. Throughout this story she showed little energy. I kept telling her that I respected how important this was to her, but that from my perspective there was no life in it; it wasn't real. As she got more and more frustrated, she began to go deeper. As this point, I had her hold her belly. As she spoke of her confusion and pain, it would be softer. The moment she talked about her career plans, her sense that she needed to leave the marriage, her abstract ideas about the cancer and about what she needed to do for healing, her belly became hard. I kept reminding her to watch this. She found that she could not talk about herself in this latter way and allow her belly to remain soft. But when it was soft, she could feel warmth moving through her body and sense an aliveness within her.

Now, perhaps there is just as much "reality" in the space of lowered bodily aliveness as there is in that of greater bodily energy. But, from my experience, a state of greater bodily radiance tends to embrace more of our being. However, it may not seem as rational or coherent a space. It is more difficult to describe and far more vulnerable to relate from. Thus, it may seem to be less conscious, but it is not. I call this space, "speaking from the heart." We took the experiment a step deeper. I had her husband lie next to her in a full-length embrace. She was to keep a part of her awareness in her belly so that she could notice when it got tense. As soon as they embraced, her belly hardened. (In all fairness, to embrace one's spouse in front of other people can be embarrassing.) But, when she could let the belly get soft, in this vulnerable position, there was more energy flowing through her than when she had been able to do this by herself. Every time there came a suggestion to merge more deeply with her husband, her belly tightened. It became clear that she had excluded, quite unconsciously, all the energy from her marriage. She was unwilling to meet him unguardedly, and thus the heightened life force that can come through the merging process was not available to her. Her reasons for this exclusion might have been "right," but she was shutting down her own life force to accomplish this separation. She was trying to fill this gap by pouring more energy into her career and into her life philosophy. While this did hold value for her, from the level of her bodily energies it was a lower, more controlled and bounded state.

She practiced lying next to her husband and allowing her belly to become completely unguarded. She saw that this increased the energy she felt, but she resented having to work with him to find this greater vibrancy. In reality, she wasn't using him; he just symbolized a place where she had shut down her energetic openness and created a barrier against life in order to sustain and make herself less vulnerable. Rather than lose herself into the larger energy that results through loving communion, she had unconsciously accepted a more bounded state of lowered energy and aliveness. And she wasn't even aware of this (as none of us ordinarily are). She was aware only of her reasons for not letting herself go—and it was not only with her husband, it was with everyone.

I began gently tapping parts of her body. I could touch her shoulders, her arms, or her legs, and her belly would remain relaxed. But the moment I touched her head, her belly tensed and she closed down. Touching her there brought her to thinking, and this activity shut down her energy flow and separated her from awareness of her own body. We practiced this until she could remain open while her husband held her and I tapped her. Then I tapped the area where the cancer was. Immediately she shut down even more than before. As soon as she did, she no longer wanted to lie near him. The whole thing became foolish, an embarrassment, an invasion of her privacy. Precisely. She could die with her privacy or learn to release it and perhaps find new aliveness.

We stayed with this until they could snuggle comfortably and I could touch her breast area near the tumor and she could still keep her belly open. At this point, there was almost a flame of energy pouring through her and radiating from her. It is hard to describe this in any other way. But clearly much more of her was present to her experience.

At the end of this sharing, she was in a very different consciousness; she was more available, more present, and easier to approach. I hoped that she would be able to continue this exploration and that by using her own belly as a kind of feedback doorway for openness she could keep returning to a more energized awareness.

Even if we are given a key to wholeness, it doesn't mean we will use it. The real key was not that her belly could signal when she contracted and shut down. The key was that unobstructed relating is a much fuller state of being. Our bodies are in fact doors to an infinite potential.

By experimenting with the humming exercise, it is possible to develop a sense of when your own body is more open to energy. Just notice the quality of your awareness as you settle into the humming and being to sense your abdomen. Learn to let your abdomen become relaxed and unguarded and become aware of your abdomen during the course of the day. If some other part of your body feels more appropriate as the feedback doorway, then work with that area. But once you have determined which part of your body most fully reflects your state of awareness (particularly, the knowledge of being connected to a larger sense of self), practice tuning in to this part. It will tell you the truth of your energy and your level of openness or contractedness. I can't help recalling the Buddha and other wise men with their wonderful, round, unencumbered bellies and laughing faces.

4.

MOVEMENT AND VOICE MEDITATIONS

THESE MEDITATIONS ARE AMONG the most important you can explore, especially when working to heighten body energies and facilitate deep rebalancing. They do require a greater commitment than more sedentary meditations and may be harder to motivate yourself to do. Before reading the Commentary, I recommend that you first try them on your own.

Assuming you are able to walk and can find a place where you will be free to move and make noise, you can readily experiment with these meditations. If there is no place outdoors where you can be alone and feel unencumbered, you can certainly do them in your own home.

Step 1. In your own home, select a piece of music. You can choose from many different kinds. Some may feel too inhibiting, while others are too familiar. Popular disco dance music is often very good because the beat is steady and we are accustomed to it. On the other hand, familiarity is also a limitation; the feeling communicated by the music tends to stimulate a repetitive disco-type movement and a lot of old memories. Since the object of this meditation is to allow moments when the movement becomes completely uninhibited and spontaneous, possibly with fresh and unique expression, familiar music can be an obstacle. Sometimes a dynamic symphony can be good. (See the list of music included with Door 2, Listening to Music.)

Begin to bounce up and down to the beat of the music. Make sure you have enough space, because it helps to keep your eyes closed. Breathe deeply at first, even exaggerating your breathing. On a scale of 1 to 10, allow your initial movements to be in the 3 to 4 range so that you are warming up but not exhausting yourself too quickly. As you jump up and down to the music, let your arms be like rubber bands responding to the bodily actions of bouncing up and down. Let them become so loose that they are just flapping around like the arms of a straw doll. Play with this and let the sense of being a straw doll or a puppet increase. Let this spread into the whole movement so that more and more of you is like a puppet — loose, unselfconscious, even silly.

Then imagine someone is above you with a set of strings that are jiggling you around to the music. Become more and more elastic, more and more surrendered to the puppeteer. Imagine that the puppeteer is trying to get you to express the energy of the music. This is why it is important that the music have differing rhythms, feelings, and intensities. It isn't just a process of dancing "as if" you were a puppet. Rather, the image of a puppet is used to suggest that, letting go of images or memories, you give your body over to the moment in new ways, as though you were letting something else move you.

Whenever you find yourself thinking about what you are doing, return your awareness to the space above your head where the strings are moving you around, and let your movements become more and more free. If this carries you into a movement other than bouncing, that is fine.

Continue matching your movements to the quality of the music. When it is soft, you become soft. When it is strong and powerful, you are the embodiment of strength and fullness.

Relax past the space where you think, "The music is strong, so I'll dance harder." Instead, just feel into the music with your whole being and move toward that space where there is no mental mediation between the quality of the music and the energy of your movement. We all know these kinds of moments: when you do something perfectly without thinking, or when something you have practiced for a long time happens effortlessly. Every time you become self-conscious, imagine that something above your head is controlling the movements. Keep letting go so that your body begins to move in new ways. After a while, shift the center of the movement from the space above your head to other places. What happens when you move from the chest or the lower abdomen? Explore.

If you find that you are too self-conscious, imagine yourself in different roles. You might be a drum majorette leading the marching band, or a person made of jelly, or a boxer, or tumbleweed blowing in the wind, or a celestial sculptor carving the sky. These are just suggestions, but the moment an image of yourself in some role enters your mind, let the movement go with the image. Explore the space where body and mind are creating simultaneously.

The more lost you become in the dancing, the more energy you can bring to it without being exhausted. But sometimes, in order to get out of a rut and find a new sense of freedom, it is good to push for a while. So take the strength and vitality that you are putting into the dance up to 8 or briefly 9. From time to time, give it all the energy you can, but for short periods only. When you are tired, don't stop. Rather, allow yourself to settle into a less taxing movement. Sometimes a new level of absorption into the movement occurs after such full effort.

Learn to let go of trying. Turn the movement over to a higher power and let it move you. If this "meditation" isn't turned into work and just becomes a new kind of play, it can be very empowering.

Dance and move like this for about twenty minutes, or until the music ends, if you are physically able. Make sure in advance that the music is not too brief. If you find yourself wanting to stop before the music stops (which invariably happens), don't stop; stay with it, moving gently until you have forgotten that you want to stop. If you again realize that you want to stop, dance a little more, letting go of the urge to stop. Only stop when the music stops. When I was exploring this particular process, I worked several mornings a week with Beethoven's Fifth Symphony, which lasts about thirty-five minutes.

Obviously, some readers are not going to be physically capable of doing this kind of movement. However, rather than be discouraged, try something a little different. Put on the music and let the process happen in your mind. Visualize yourself moving to the music. Be as free and outrageous as you can. If while you are in bed, your hands and arms can move, and your toes can wiggle, then bring them into the experience. The most important things are to let go of self-consciousness and to allow your body to move spontaneously so as to have as much of your being (body, fantasies, feeling state) as possible converged in a single dynamic experience.

Step 2. This is a natural extension of the first process. It developed spontaneously after my experience of the consciousness shift.

I would go for walks and find myself humming or singing. Soon I would be dancing to my own improvised song. Then the song would be reflecting from the environment a sense of life and of the world. I would be carried beyond myself and all of a sudden everything was just effortless, meditative, silent. Sometimes before I began these walks into the inner life, I would feel as if I were coming down with a cold or as if I were lost and confused. Afterwards I would notice that the cold was gone and a wonderful sense of peace and health permeated my body. Simultaneously, I was aware of the Divine. I felt that I had returned to holy ground. Once again everything would become sacred, and I would be reminded to give thanks for life. I would return home propelled with new strength and clarity of purpose. It was these early experiences which began to "inform" my life and eventually became much of the basis of the transformational conference work.

✿

Begin to sing a simple tune to yourself. Keep exploring the tune, elaborating it in simple ways so that it has a natural coherence. If you are at home, begin to walk around your most spacious room so that your walk creates a tempo for the song. Of course the best place for exploring this meditation is outdoors on some hiking trail, wooded walk, or beach–any place where you have space and a sense of freedom. Let the walk establish or support the rhythm of the song that is emerging from you.

It is fine to start with a tune you know, but try to let it have a flavor that is characteristic of your mood. If you are feeling jaunty, then let the tune, even a Christmas carol, be sassy and jaunty. If your are feeling heavy and deep, then let the tune mirror your mood. Stay with the tune until it begins to have a life of its own. Play with it until you like it. Again, I suggest a simple song involving only a few notes so that you can modify it in easy ways and let it come to life. Repeat it over and over. It doesn't have to be a song by anyone's standards but yours. Again, as soon as you begin to get a feel for the song, so that it has a life of its own, let the pace of your walking create a tempo for your song.

If it feels right, let your hands participate by clapping or snapping fingers. Let the hands and arms augment the rhythm and feeling of the song and carry you into a deeper involvement. Finally, just begin to dance to your own song. Keep singing, finger snapping, arm waving, shoulder dipping, swooping, swaying–whatever allows you to augment the energy and aliveness of the song by joining it with the body. Imagine that you are so full in your song and dance that people and animals have gathered around and are being drawn into it with you.

At this point it is difficult for me to suggest much more about this process. It is possible to become totally absorbed in the song and dance. It is possible to improvise new sounds and new rhythms, and to fall effortlessly into one feeling after another. It is possible to let your whole being become a celebration. Just play with this exercise and let go of trying to do it in any particular way. Trust that you already know what I am talking about and have felt it at other times in your life and just give yourself over to this play.

Step 3. Step 3 is really just a variation on Step 2. It involves standing or sitting alone somewhere you feel safe. This time the exploration is more deeply into the voice.

Begin by intoning a note or sound (sounds with musical quality tend to open into larger spaces, but it may feel more appropriate to start with a noise, or perhaps a wail), and sustain it for as long as comfortable. Repeat this again and again. At a certain point move your awareness out toward the ceiling or into the trees around you or into the sky and listen to your sound from that point of awareness. Begin to experiment with the voice, moving it from one sound to another, one tone to another. Experiment with these qualities: fullness, low pitch, high pitch, roundness, nasal sound, chesty sound, richness, thinness. Make your note rounder, more chesty, lower, higher, and so on. Allow the sounds to flow from one quality to another as smoothly as possible, so that you hardly notice it shifting. Imagine that there is a hushed audience using the sound (and the energy or consciousness that is being carried by your sound) as a meditation. Make sure that the people in the back of the auditorium can hear you. Explore softness, but try to produce the quiet sound with a fullness or richness. As you let the sounds shift in loudness and other qualities, begin to flow the notes into a theme or song and let it carry a feeling. It will have its own feeling; all you have to do is recognize it and join it to make it fuller. Extend the boundary of the sounding/singing until it becomes a force for expressing more and more of your heart and soul in that moment.

When you become aware of what you are doing, notice how

you are feeling. From time to time stop for a while and just look around. Then close your eyes and begin again. Explore this for as long as it feels good.

Step 4. Repeat Step 3 with a friend. The key here is not to go along merely making your sound while your friend makes his or hers. Take turns leading each other into different types of sounds, different rhythms, and different feeling states. Explore following each other and then become the leader. Let the leading or following dynamic occur spontaneously. Even as you are making a sound, sense how it feels and coordinates with the sound that your partner is making. At no point should you be totally involved in what only you are doing and disconnected from what your partner is doing. At the same time, don't become so absorbed in the other sound that you lose a sense of your own. Explore the possibility of sharing or merging your awareness into each other.

In this exercise, there is no time frame. I recommend you both agree that when you are thinking, "Now it's time to stop," you don't stop. Trust that if you just let go into the sharing, it will reach a point where it stops on its own. In fact, it can stop in such a way that you know it is stopping and yet you are not thinking that it should.

Commentary

Our bodies are not rational! We cannot explain them and therefore nothing we do that involves our bodies (which is virtually everything we do) can ever by reduced to a rational explanation. This may come as a surprise to many, for surely we live as though things can be made sense of—especially our bodies. But the truth is that even now as you are reading, you don't know how your hand reaches out and turns the page. We can dissect the physiological processes involved, but ultimately we do not know how the thought is formulated that tells the body to make this movement.

In this sense, our bodies are non-rational, and so is everything we do with them. Notice, I did not say "irrational," which implies disturbance or imbalance. Ordinarily we impose reason on our bodies even as we develop an ego. We demand that our bodies do certain things and train them to do so. The things the body can do and the sense of "me" are inseparable. But the body is far more than what we can make it do, and far more than the "me" who participates in this doing. We seem to know as much about the human body as we do about the universe, and that is very, very little.

It is no wonder, then, that when we approach illness, we try to work with the body as though it were a rational system. We think that if we can only figure out what is needed, and do the right thing, then we will get the desired results. This is true within certain limits. But if you want to know physical health you must get out of the way and allow something non-reasonable to happen with the body. It is precisely at this non-reasonableness that these exercises are directed.

Think for a moment of your experience with medicine. You wait to be seen, then you speak, the doctor examines you, you are given a prescription, and then you go home. It appears so incredibly rational. It seems so sensible. But this fragmentary experience is directed first at one and then another piece of your life. When have you had a moment to be at-one with yourself? When have you had a chance to be at-one with your whole body, humming and singing in aliveness? (I suppose we are at-one when we are asleep, and this is a regenerative time, but unless we are carefully prepared to join the healing potential of dreams, sleep only minimally translates into wholeness and aliveness in our waking state. We go to sleep and forget our pain, our disease, our fear, but we do not become unified.)

The dancing and singing exercises utilize the essential non-rationality of the body and make possible moments when we can become at-one in extended aliveness. Throughout the exploration of such exercises we come up against the boundary-making mechanism of our mind. This is the one that says, "I don't want to do this. I can't do this. I want to stop, I would rather do something else, I should be doing . . . ." Notice your protests, but don't succumb to them. To do so sets up a boundary you cannot go beyond. It is essential to learn to play at the edge of these relative boundaries. It is not a question of pushing your limits, of challenging yourself in a do-or-die dynamic. It is a much more gentle, even tender, exploration of how one level of our being and its energetic dynamic will impose a reality upon us and how we can learn to go beyond this.

The exercises are really celebrations of life in the moment. When the part of ourselves that wants to stop separates us from our experience, we have an opportunity to move through it. Notice that I said "move through." I didn't say "repress" or "deny" it. To force ourselves onward when we want to stop, rather than let go a little more, only fosters a split within ourselves. It is better just to be aware of this process, to keep looking at it. It is almost impossible for consciousness to keep sending us the same impulse if we look right at it. In fact, if we can observe ourselves, if we can notice how this inner conflict is making us feel, if we can maintain our attention fully on this desire to stop, all of a sudden we discover that we are absorbed in the dance once again and that we never really said, "No, I won't stop!" Thus we have passed through a relative boundary that, if agreed to, would lead to limiting and lowering our energy.

As we let go in this way, we balance our energies and heighten them. I don't know the mechanism of this, but I suspect it has to do with living as if we were in many tiny compartments. When we lose ourselves in the song we become more unified and no longer obstruct the flow of a more universal energy. In a sense, we tap a higher dimension, because the whole is far, far greater than the sum of its parts. It may seem paradoxical that rational concerns that move into very technical considerations rarely lead to higher dimensions. More usually, such concerns are lived one, two, or several steps removed from the whole of ourselves. By thinking about what we need to do tomorrow, the approaching surgery, what others may be feeling, and so on, we remain in a fragmented, lower-energy state. *But we do not know it!* That is, we don't know it until we have an experience of coming into a state of unity where our physical sense, our feeling state, and the content of our thoughts have converged into a single action with lots of aliveness and vitality.

Even the idea "I am sick" is a self-definition, no matter how substantial the medical information to confirm it. The simple and wondrous fact is that there are levels of us in which we are more or less sick. Therefore, it is vital that one be willing to explore this relative idea, "I am sick." If there is resistance to exploring this, if you find yourself saying, "But, I *am* sick," and at the same time unwilling to look at whether there are other ways to experience yourself, then at least be honest and admit you must actually want to be sick. This doesn't mean that you aren't sick or that it is "all in your mind." That is much too rational a perspective to ever approach the truth! Also, it doesn't mean that if you just shift your point of view the disease will go away.

We are in that difficult territory where we have the freedom to explore ourselves, not because we are sick and something may make us well, but simply because we are alive. Therefore, let us notice how we are alive. Let us notice what we will and won't accept, what we will and won't explore. Until the moment we die we are not yet dead, and there remains the possibility to experience something more in life.

If you have found yourself resisting the idea of these exercises, look at the relative boundary limiting you. Where have you decided to stop? Why have you decided to stop? Why do we settle for the routine of our lives, so that in order to feel alive we have to travel some place else on weekends?

It is wise to examine these arbitrary routines of life, and the arbitrary boundaries we set up to keep us from entering fully into the moment. Each boundary represents a yes to the familiar and a no to the new. Each boundary represents a place of reason and a closing down of the non-rational — that unknown seemingly beyond our control. Each boundary represents a level of life force within which we have become comfortable and a separation from a larger, more universal energy. Therefore, each boundary represents a smaller, less integrated, less coherent and universally-oriented body.

The body of the person who has explored these exercises and becomes absorbed in sound and movement is a larger body, more capable of handling higher energy. Thus it is a body that knows how to regulate each part in reference to a greater wholeness. Such a body simply doesn't require the same destructive forces to break down its narrowness. Therefore, it feels differently and it feels more. Perhaps it also feels better.

5. THE ENERGY EMBRACE

Between us there is but a narrow wall,
And by sheer chance, for it would take merely a
  call from your lips or mine to break it down,
And that without a sound.

R. M. RILKE
Book of Hours
"You, Neighbor, God"

THE ENERGY EMBRACE IS A WAY of relating that can become profoundly enriching. We have all experienced it, but when it occurs spontaneously—following orgasm, holding each other after a period of intense stress, or soothing an infant—there is little (if any) conscious recognition of this state and its importance. It is very pleasurable, but we don't realize that it is always available. Rather, we quickly fall back into the ordinary kind of sharing that maintains our separateness. It is precisely this separation that we want to examine more closely and, to the best of our ability, transcend.

The Energy Embrace is divided into a sequence of exercises. They should be explored in order, except for the sixth, which can be done at any time after the first has been adequately practiced and understood. All the commentaries are best read *after* doing the exercises on several occasions.

1 / Finding and Entering the Space

First, find a partner who is willing to share with you. There is no reason to choose someone especially close to you. The experience can go just as deep with a stranger who is interested in exploring something new. A third person will be needed to read the instructions to the two of you.

To begin this exercise, sit comfortably next to each other. You can be facing or sitting side by side; one can be in bed, the other in a chair by the bed. It is important to be close enough to reach out and touch each other without straining.

As reader, you must pace the words at a speed that allows the listeners to follow their inner experience. You can do this by pausing and focusing inward to follow your own inner experience. Read the words as you would read poetry. Let them flow slowly and easily. In my work, I spontaneously speak the exercise to the group, using my voice and my familiarity with the material to induct the experience. Obviously, the reader may not have this background. But, if you will spend a little time reading the exercises through, sensing the rhythm and pacing, you can bring the exercise to life.

As the listeners are carried into the exercise, it is important not to get bogged down trying to understand what the words mean literally. Just move with whatever the words mean to you. It is your own experience that counts, not whether you are having the experience you think I intend. For example, I may say, "a sense of presence, of energy . . . ." You may not be feeling whatever you think I mean by "presence" or "energy," but you will be experiencing something. Stay with whatever you are experiencing. When I say, "breathe into the space . . . ," breathe into the space of whatever is happening in your awareness. If you just relax and trust that you will follow the exercise without any problem, the words will not present an obstacle; they will just suggest a way of being that will happen for you quite effortlessly and naturally.

When reading aloud, don't bother with the numbers. They are included just to indicate the progression of the exercise. After you have guided the pair into the experience, you can enter the experience with them without saying anything.

Begin reading.
(Do not read the numbers aloud.)

1. Now, close your eyes . . . . Before entering into the Energetic Embrace with someone, it is essential to look carefully at your consecration. Consecration refers to the spirit in which you give yourself to life. Silently, feel toward your consecration. Inwardly, tell yourself that this experience is offered to the Highest Good, both for yourself and anyone else who is involved. Know that you trust the deeper wisdom and wholeness, that it is guiding your unfolding. In this way, you are consciously acknowledging your already existing wholeness, even though, at the moment, you may not be directly aware of it. Energetic Embrace opens you to a vast dimension. Therefore, before letting go into the experience, KNOW that you have paused and recalled a deeper wholeness and invited it to guide you. *(pause)*

2. Notice your breathing. Watch the breath as it flows in and out. Stay with this . . . effortlessly watching the unbroken wave of breath. First in . . . then turning . . . and out . . . then turning . . . and in . . . . *(pause)*

3. Become aware of the shift in awareness that occurs as you stay with the breathing. Keep watching the breath. If the breathing changes, let it. Don't try to control or regulate the breath, just watch it. Notice the breathing as if you were watching a wild animal; you don't want to create anything that might

frighten it away. Let the touch of your awareness be very light, very subtle. (*pause*)

4. To help attune to the subtle quality aroused by gently noticing the breath, imagine that the center of your chest is porous and you are breathing in and out through it. Feel the breath as it comes in and out through this fine, porous area . . . . (*pause*)

5. Become aware of what this feels like . . . As you breathe in through this space—the porous, transparent area in the mid-chest—become exquisitely receptive. The more receptive you are to the space . . . the more exquisitely and delicately receptive . . . the larger and more substantial the space becomes . . . . As you breathe out, relax utterly into this space, sink into it, dissolve into it . . . become the space. (*pause*) The receptive in-breath gathers energy to the space within awareness . . . it seems filled with subtle feeling, subtle presence. (*pause*) As you breathe out, surrender yourself into this space. By surrendering, you are merging into the space. Sense how the space is becoming more alive as you breathe out into it. (*pause*) . . .

6. Extend this feeling by expanding the area of receptivity as you breathe in. Involve your whole upper body. (*pause*) It is as though the whole upper body were porous . . . transparent to the breath. (*pause*) Continue to let your awareness be gently and exquisitely receptive to this space as you breathe in and out through the whole upper body . . . the chest . . . the arms . . . the hands . . . . As you breathe out, actively fill the space generated by the exquisite sensitivity of the inhalation. (*pause*) . . . .

7. The breath itself has become something else . . . a vehicle for subtle feeling . . . subtle energy that is gathering and deepening within your awareness as you breathe. Stay with this awareness . . . go deeper into this subtle feeling of presence or energy. (*pause*) . . . Give yourself permission to become even more receptive to this subtle feeling . . . . Breathing out, sink into this feeling . . . merge into it . . . let go, utterly, into

it . . . . Sense it becoming fuller, stronger, breath by breath. *(pause)* . . . .

8. Now extend this process through your whole body . . . as though the whole body has become, through the breath, a door to a larger space. *(pause)* . . . .

9. Now the quantum leap. Begin to extend this sense of awareness outward, about one foot beyond the skin boundary. As before, become exquisitely receptive to this space as you inhale. The receptivity draws the energy of awareness to the space so that it becomes filled with a subtle presence . . . filled with a gentle energy. *(pause)* . . . As you breathe out, sense your own breath as a presence that fills this space. In this way, you are beginning to empower a field of energy around the body. Stay with this presence within and around the body. Let it get as deep as it can. *(pause)* . . . .

10. If you become aware of thoughts, or are distracted by them, allow your awareness of these thoughts to just relax. It doesn't matter what the content is. Imagine that your awareness has grabbed these thoughts firmly and that is why they are so strong. Now just let the grip relax; let your hand open; let the grasp of your awareness become softer and softer. Do not fight the thoughts; let them be. Just let the grasp of your awareness become softer and softer . . . . The thoughts or other distractions will change of themselves. Let them dissolve away like the mist off dry ice. Gently, return to the breath and the space within and around the body . . . . Gently return to the sense of this space . . . its subtle aliveness . . . subtle presence. *(pause)* . . . .

11. Extend this field-of-awareness until it encompasses the person with whom you are sharing. Become aware that she(he) is inside this space, that she(he) is an intrinsic part of this extended field of awareness, not something separate . . . . Become exquisitely receptive to this enlarged space which includes the other. *(pause)* . . . . As you breathe in, the realness and depth of the space grows. As you breath into it, you give more of the

energy of awareness to it and it becomes more substantial, more filled with subtle presence. Let the exhalation join you to this space. As you breathe out, merge with the space. (pause) Stay with this exploration . . . with each breath becoming more receptive, falling more deeply into the space, and filling it with presence . . . . Sense yourself breathing and drawing awareness to the space within you and around you. Your partner is a part of this awareness, not someone separate or "outside" of you. Rest gently in the richness of this space. (pause for five or ten minutes)

12. Now it is time to return to more ordinary awareness. Begin to withdraw the sense of presence that is the space within you and around you. (pause) Become aware of the skin boundry. (pause) Become aware of the air going in and out of your lungs. (pause) Tell yourself that you are ready and willing to return to ordinary awareness. (pause) Open your eyes. Notice how your body feels. Notice your thoughts. Is the mind quiet, or active?

This ends the first part of the Energy Embrace exploration.

13. If it feels appropriate, you can begin to share your experience verbally with your partner. However, please do not try to explain the experience. You may find interesting similarities in some of what you each experienced, but there is no need to give this much significance. Above all, don't compare. Most important, notice the quality of your awareness. Again, don't interpret this. If you feel exhilarated, relaxed, or tired, just notice. There is no right way to feel. (pause for ten minutes maximum)

14. After having verbally shared for a maximum of ten minutes, stop the discussion. Notice your awareness. How has the awareness changed since disengaging from the Energy Embrace? (reader stops)

Commentary

Most of the time, the Energy Embrace is going to be explored with someone we know. But we can learn a great deal about ourselves by noticing whether we would prefer to explore the Energy Embrace with a person we don't know well or with someone with whom we have been involved for a long time.

When we choose someone we know, we have to first release what we know about the person in order to go into the essentially experiential, nonrational space in which Energy Embrace occurs. In order to merge awareness with a familiar partner, we have to be willing to let go of what we know, think, or feel about the person, for what we know is always limited and conditional. Thus what we know actually separates us. A familiar partner may make us comfortable in that we know who we are relative to him (because we think we know who he is), but from the perspective of the energy that can be awakened as we share, these ideas act as a damper. In short, we have to let go of the part of ourselves that knows, thinks and feels in this way. With a stranger, we have to release the assumption that in order to come close to people we must know and trust them. Often we feel safe with someone we know—perhaps it will not be safe with a stranger. On the other hand, with a stranger we may feel peculiarly free to be new in ourselves.

In the Energy Embrace, the obstacles of familiarity and nonfamiliarity are really the same thing. By having a preference we have already set up a subtle limitation to the depth of sharing. Deep energy and love is possible between any of us if we are willing to let go of that particular level of our being where preference is rooted. Such a step already implies a significant expansion in consciousness and greatly enhances opportunity to be enlivened more deeply and in many situations. Then we discover that the depth of energy we share as we embrace depends on the depth to which we know ourselves. It is a depth of knowing that comes from how we have lived and how we have been undone by life.

2 / The Quality of the Energy

(The reader begins by guiding the pair once again through steps 1 through 11 of the previous exercise, repeated here. Then the exploration continues directly into the following steps.)

1. Now, close your eyes . . . . Before entering into the Energetic Embrace with someone, it is essential to look carefully at your consecration. Consecration refers to the spirit in which you give yourself to life. Silently, feel toward your consecration. Inwardly, tell yourself that this experience is offered to the Highest Good, both for yourself and anyone else who is involved. Know that you trust the deeper wisdom and wholeness, that it is guiding your unfolding. In this way, you are consciously acknowledging your already existing wholeness, even though, at the moment, you may not be directly aware of it. Energetic Embrace opens you to a vast dimension. Therefore, before letting go into the experience, KNOW that you have paused and recalled a deeper wholeness and invited it to guide you. *(pause)*

2. Notice your breathing. Watch the breath as it flows in and out. Stay with this . . . effortlessly watching the unbroken wave of breath. First in . . . then turning . . . and out . . . then turning . . . and in . . . . *(pause)*

3. Become aware of the shift in awareness that occurs as you stay with the breathing. Keep watching the breath. If the breathing changes, let it. Don't try to control or regulate the breath, just watch it. Notice the breathing as if you were watching a wild animal; you don't want to create anything that might frighten it away. Let the touch of your awareness be very light, very subtle. *(pause)*

4. To help attune to the subtle quality aroused by gently noticing the breath, imagine that the center of your chest is porous and you are breathing in and out through it. Feel the breath as it comes in and out through this fine, porous area . . . . *(pause)*

5. Become aware of what this feels like . . . As you breathe in through this space—the porous, transparent area in the mid-

chest—become exquisitely receptive. The more receptive you are to the space . . . the more exquisitely and delicately receptive . . . the larger and more substantial the space becomes . . . . As you breath out, relax utterly into this space, sink into it, dissolve into it . . . become the space. *(pause)* The receptive in-breath gathers energy to the space within awareness . . . it seems filled with subtle feeling, subtle presence. *(pause)* As you breathe out, surrender yourself into this space. By surrendering, you are merging into the space. Sense how the space is becoming more alive as you breathe out into it. *(pause)*

6. Extend this feeling by expanding the area of receptivity as you breathe in. Involve your whole upper body. *(pause)* It is as though the whole upper body were porous . . . transparent to the breath. *(pause)* Continue to let your awareness be gently and exquisitely receptive to this space as you breathe in and out through the whole upper body . . . the chest . . . the arms . . . the hands . . . . As you breathe out, actively fill the space generated by the exquisite sensitivity of the inhalation. *(pause)* . . . .

7. The breath itself has become something else . . . a vehicle for subtle feeling . . . subtle energy that is gathering and deepening within your awareness as you breathe. Stay with this awareness . . . go deeper into this subtle feeling of presence or energy. *(pause)* . . . Give yourself permission to become even more receptive to this subtle feeling . . . . Breathing out, sink into this feeling . . . merge into it . . . let go, utterly, into it . . . . Sense it becoming fuller, stronger, breath by breath. *(pause)* . . . .

8. Now extend this process through your whole body . . . as though the whole body has become, through the breath, a door to a larger space. *(pause)* . . . .

9. Now the quantum leap. Begin to extend this sense of awareness outward, about one foot beyond the skin boundary. As before, become exquisitely receptive to this space as you inhale. The receptivity draws the energy of awareness to the space so that it becomes filled with a subtle presence . . . filled with a

gentle energy. *(pause)* . . . As you breathe out, sense your own breath as a presence that fills this space. In this way, you are beginning to empower a field of energy around the body. Stay with this presence within and around the body. Let it get as deep as it can. *(pause)* . . . .

10. If you become aware of thoughts, or are distracted by them, allow your awareness of these thoughts to just relax. It doesn't matter what the content is. Imagine that your awareness has grabbed these thoughts firmly and that is why they are so strong. Now just let the grip relax; let your hand open; let the grasp of your awareness become softer and softer. Do not fight the thoughts; let them be. Just let the grasp of your awareness become softer and softer . . . . The thoughts or other distractions will change of themselves. Let them dissolve away like the mist off dry ice. Gently, return to the breath and the space within and around the body . . . . Gently return to the sense of this space . . . its subtle aliveness . . . subtle presence.
(pause) . . . .

11. Extend this field-of-awareness until it encompasses the person with whom you are sharing. Become aware that she(he) is inside this space, that she(he) is an intrinsic part of this extended field of awareness, not something separate . . . . Become exquisitely receptive to this enlarged space which includes the other. *(pause)* . . . . As you breathe in, the realness and depth of the space grows. As you breath into it, you give more of the energy of awareness to it and it becomes more substantial, more filled with subtle presence. Let the exhalation join you to this space. As you breathe out, merge with the space. *(pause)* Stay with this exploration . . . with each breath becoming more receptive, falling more deeply into the space, and filling it with presence . . . . Sense yourself breathing and drawing awareness to the space within you and around you. Your partner is a part of this awareness, not someone separate or "outside" of you. Rest gently in the richness of this space. *(pause for five or ten minutes)*

12. Now we will begin to transmute the quality of the em-

brace to a finer energy. To do so, our relationship to the moment must become even more surrendered and unconditional. Sense into the presence within and around you in which your partner is contained. Begin to offer this awareness to a higher potential.

As you breathe in, allow a sense of "yes." It is a yes to the moment, a yes to life *(pause)* . . . . Feel your heart melting with each yes. Feel it opening to embrace existence. *(pause)* . . . . With each breath, allow this to become a sense of celebration. *(pause)* . . . .

13. As you breathe in, become exquisitely sensitive to the depth, the fineness, the purity of yes. It is as though your whole being is becoming a living prayer. *(pause)* . . . . With each out-breath, sense your awareness flowing out into this shared space, deepening it, adding energy and presence to it. *(pause)* . . . . Become totally open to the presence that is filling the space of awareness. As you breathe in, refine this presence by imaging it to be the purest energy, the finest love. *(pause)* . . . . The more receptive you become to it, the finer it becomes . . . and, as you again enter awareness with the exhalation, your breath delicately but actively merges with this awareness and empowers it . . . becomes fuller . . . more palpable. *(pause)* . . . .

14. Let the sense of celebration become as fine, as simple, as effortless as it can, breath by breath, moment by moment . . . . When self-consciousness returns, when awareness of the surroundings or of your partner as separate arises . . . celebrate this . . . say yes to this . . . let the awareness dissolve into the sense of presence . . . . Stay with this for awhile, exploring this space. *(Reader: At this point allow yourself to relax and stay quietly present while the partners continue in this space. There should be no more directions for five to ten minutes. You may continue with Exercise 3, Energy Transfer at this time and omit the five- to ten-minute pause and Step 15.)*

15. Now it is time to return to more ordinary awareness. Begin to withdraw the sense of presence that is the space within you and around you. *(pause)* Become aware of the skin boun-

dary. (*pause*) Become aware of the air going in and out of your lungs. (*pause*) Tell yourself that you are ready and willing to return to ordinary awareness. (*pause*) Open your eyes. Notice how your body feels. Notice your thoughts. Is the mind quiet, or active?

Once again, take a few minutes for sharing.

3 / Energy Transfer

(*If you have stopped and rested after doing Exercise 2 or if it is a new day, please start at the beginning of Exercise 2 to do this Energy Transfer exercise.*)

1. Notice your breathing once again (*pause*) On the in-breath, sense your awareness opening to the finest quality of energy, an unconditional yes . . . feel it gathering within your field of awareness like a fine mist, a fine presense . . . . As you exhale, sense this gathered presence flowing out from you, particularly down your arms and out your hands. Let the exhalation be slow, so that you feel the breath as a current flowing out from your whole energy field and particularly from the hands. Stay with this and let the sense of flow gently enhance, breath by breath. (*pause*) . . . .

2. Be aware of the sense of flow . . . awareness of it increases it. Ask that the quality of energy you sense flowing through you be the finest possible. Open to this thought—"I have nothing to give or receive except Love"—and sense what this does to the quality of the energy flowing within, around, and through you. (*pause*) . . . .

3. Bring your hands together so that the palms are facing and as if there was a small ball held between them. (*pause*) . . . . As you inhale become aware of the energy gathering to you, and aware of the space between your hands . . . as you exhale, let the energy flow and fill this space between your hands. (*pause*) . . . . Feel what happens as you push your hands softly toward each other while you exhale . . . what does it feel like to pull

them apart while you inhale? *(pause)* .... Stay with this until there is a strong, almost magnetic feeling between the hands. *(pause)* ....

4. Now, gently and slowly reach out with your hands so that you can touch your partner any place that is comfortable for you to reach. (You may want to open your eyes briefly) .... As soon as your hand is about to touch your partner, hold it gently away from his or her body surface so that you are not actually making physical contact. With your hand in this position, begin to attune to the sense of presence ... as you breathe in, sense the finest energy gathering within your awareness ... as you breath out, let this presence flow gently out from your hands. *(pause)* ....

5. *(Reader: The way that you read the next section is crucial. Read it through several times until you begin to feel rapport with the space it is evoking. If you find yourself feeling a little dreamy, or if you begin to sense your own energy or awareness becoming altered, then probably you will be able to convey this passage in a valuable way. Do your best, and thank you.)*

As you breathe in, your whole being is attuned to the finest quality of energy, the deepest yes to Life, but you are also exquisitely aware of the space around you, particularly around your hand .... As you breath out, this energy flows from you, out from your hand into the space that is your partner .... Just as you did with the energy between your own hands, sense the energy connection to your partner. *(pause)* .... You can let your hand touch him lightly, but keep breathing beyond the sense of physical touch and into the sense of subtle touch occurring through the energy that is flowing through you .... Let the energy be as fine as it can be .... Once again, feel this thought ... "I have nothing to give, nothing to receive, except Love." *(pause)* ....

You can move your hand to another place on your partner. Before making very light physical touch, sense the energetic connection. You don't have to touch at all if you don't feel like it. **Now here is the key. Let go of the idea that you are send-**

ing energy or doing something to your partner. Rather, sense the energetic connection you feel as you make subtle contact and, instead of trying to send more energy to your partner, give over to the perfect wholeness of the moment. Let the connection to your partner and the sense of your relationship to Life become the same thing! . . . . Let the breath continue to connect you to the sense of presence . . . breathing in, exquisitely receptive to the perfect wholeness of the moment . . . sensing this awareness gathering within and around you as a presence . . . breathing out and deepening this sense . . . feel the energetic connection to your partner through your hands and through your whole field of awareness . . . . Now, letting the whole space . . . all of it . . . become one single space of celebration, of devotion to Life . . . . (Stay in this space for five minutes.)

6. Now begin to release the connection to your partner. Gently withdraw your awareness from your hands. Draw your field of awareness back so that your partner is "outside" you once again. Become aware of your own body and your own physical boundaries. Tell yourself that you are ready to open your eyes; do so, when you feel ready. Stay quiet for a few minutes and just notice how you feel. Notice the quality of your awareness, the activity of your thoughts, the feeling in your body, the appearance of the room. *(pause)* . . . .

7. Take about ten minutes to share your experiences with each other and to acknowledge each other. Once again, try not to get analytical and comparative.

Commentary

The key to refining and expanding in the Energy Embrace is to maintain a sense of relationship to the person with whom you are sharing, even as you join your awareness with the sense of Wholeness, or the Divine Yes. This is why I say that the relationship to Existence or to God and the relationship to anyone else is the same thing. It is, "Love God with all thy heart, soul, and strength" coupled with, "Love thy neighbor as thyself."(8)

Over and over again, in my exploration of the Energy Embrace, the sense of the Divine became Everything, and simultaneously, the person with whom I was sharing ceased to exist as someone separate from me. We became One in that Presence, that palpable Aliveness. If your partner seems separate and outside, an object of your awareness, then you have not released deeply and the sense of presence in minimal. As you make the gesture of letting go with all of your being into the Wholeness of Life, the "other" person too is carried into this rarified energy. For, "others" exist, at least as far as we know, as an aspect of our own awareness, an object of our consciousness. When we allow our consciousness to give itself over into a Greater Consciousness, this objective sense of "me" and "you" gives way to a Presence, and it is through this Presence that we simultaneously embrace each other and the Wholeness of Life without a sense of separation and otherness.

What are the implications of such sharing? At first it is unclear. There is a sense of entering an altered state of consciousness, but perhaps this is occurring only within our subjective awareness. However, if we continue to pursue this exploration, we gradually discover the powerful transformative potential that exists.

Quite commonly, the Energetic Embrace itself produces a calmness or inner silence, and a new sense of rapport and fellowship. We may feel a fine vibration (what I call "molecular aliveness") within the body; it may be generalized, or focused in specific areas like the head, chest, or abdomen. There may be other subtle new sensations. The hands may feel warm and tingly, especially when we begin to use them to channel energy. There may be spontaneous tears and waves of emotion. Almost invariably, some degree of healing occurs, be it physical or psychological. Sometimes, as we have seen, this can be profound; other times it is minimal. Clearly, to enter into the sacred meditation of sharing the embrace of Life with one another as a single Wholeness is fundamentally healthy. At times, the Energetic Embrace will become so profound that a whole new sense of the mystery and holiness of life awakens, and this, beyond any of the incidental healing, is its real significance. It transforms our sense of humanness.

The Energy Embrace is not just a technique for coming into subtle relationship so that we can learn to transfer healing energy. It is an exploration of relationship, of aliveness, and the mystery of consciousness. It begins to free us from the problem-solution formula that plagues all healing endeavors with roots in the old, limited consciousness. In fact, wherever we have turned energy-sharing dynamics into specific forms (Touch for Health, Reiki, polarity massage), we have, in one sense, already missed the point. We have created another kind of separation, the healer/healed, therapist/ client split. We have taken new territory and fitted it into an old, "safe" form. We have created another situation in which to let ourselves get a *little* larger, a *little* more open. Such therapeutic forms "work," but the Energy Embrace experience, in whatever form it takes, shows how much more aliveness and depth of rapport is possible in any relationship.

In the Energy Embrace, we are unconditionally celebrating the Wholeness of Life. It is a ritual to teach us that we are always energetically embracing everyone and everything. We have only to become conscious of this. Moreover, any person able to transcend the limitations of ordinary awareness alters the reality perceived by others. This shows that "reality"— whatever else it is—is a shared consciousness.

The implications for health and for the wholeness of all life are extraordinary. I can say from experience that much of how we perceive and experience our own bodies in sickness or in health has to do with our level of consciousness and the consciousness of those with whom we share. If a person in pain comes into a room of people who offer relationship at the level of the Energy Embrace (not as formal ritual, but as a natural and ordinary understanding of life), the pain may simply disappear. The person may feel his or her body to be entirely new, or at least very different. Moods and concerns at a psychological level are suddenly irrelevant because he is feeling better. Digestion, sleep patterns, metabolism, vitality, moods, thinking, creativity—in short, every aspect of what it means to be human—will alter. It will even alter in the laboratory; test results will change.

I have seen enough of this kind of transformation to know that it is a fact, but because the level of consciousness throughout humanity as a whole so widely differs, there are very few environments that consistently maintain a higher, more inclusive energy. This is a difficult premise to test scientifically because, at the level that Energy Embrace awakens us, we are not separable; we are all part of one greater Aliveness that cannot be reduced to simple cause/effect patterns. However, I predict that over the next few years we will see increasing evidence that wherever human beings live with a greater sense of energetic rapport, a greater capacity to love, to merge and share their aliveness, such communities will have a generally enhanced health. The fact is that we can't really speak about the body, or personal reality on any level, without taking into consideration the Field of Awareness, the quality of Presence, that pervades our way of life.

Thus, one might begin an experiment with limiting the amount of time in ordinary social exchange and agree that, for every hour spent talking with someone, an equivalent time will be spent in the Energy Embrace. What would happen to your awareness, to your sense of energy flow and vitality? Actually, you may feel quite tired if you pursue the Energy Embrace for long periods until you learn how to handle the level of energy it evokes. This process of "handling," which is really an integration and transformation, will eventually involve your whole life.

If a person were to spend one hour a day in this form of sharing, his whole life would transform! It would happen gradually, but inexorably, sometimes wondrously and sometimes painfully. No one can enter this space for even an hour a day and remain unchanged. We can begin to see why we spend so much of our time chattering; it is easier and requires less of us. But as we explore the Energy Embrace, gradually learning to increase our time in this space, our overall energy level is heightened and we become more sensitive to the space within and around us. This greater sensitivity is the refinement of consciousness.

Ordinary relating is well below the threshold of our full potential for aliveness. In our ordinary relations, we maintain so much separation that very little life force is activated. Perhaps the single greatest cause of mediocrity and poor health in our world is lazy socializing! We are just unconscious that every relationship with another person is sacred! We are all healing ourselves and everyone around us to the extent that we are unobstructedly available to the deeper aliveness. Life force is activated and refined within each of us in proportion to our openness and energetic availability. When love, celebration, and that deep yes to Existence pervades our relationships, we are already engendering wholeness and health, whatever we may be doing.

The current of energy that courses through the body as we merge into a more unified awareness is tremendous. It becomes a sacred space of sharing and empowerment. To enter this space together leads to higher understanding and greater aliveness. It becomes a way of life in which the very road to God is in our relationship to each other.

4 / Group Sharing

The Embrace is now extended to include family or friends who are willing to participate. The fact is that loved ones want to help and often don't know how. Here they can contribute immensely, and they too will grow. The greatest potential for full recovery and transformation occurs when we are at our fullest and finest energy; it becomes significant not to waste the energetic potential of those who are around us most often.

Explain to them that they can learn to direct energy so that it will enrich everyone. Remember to tell them that idle socializing, while pleasant and emotionally supportive, can also be draining. Ask them to join you in the exploration of this inspiring and holy space.

1. Arrange yourselves so that hands can be linked to form a closed circle. Everyone should be comfortable, and it is good to keep eyes closed. Let the hands touch very lightly.

2. (Reader: The following is an invocation or group prayer to establish the energy for the sharing. The example given below is only a suggestion of the spirit and quality in which to consecrate this sharing. An alternative consecration can be composed extemporaneously by anyone who has a feeling to do so.)

Before going any further let us offer this sharing to the highest potential. Let us allow our awareness to relax and open to a more universal consciousness. Let us invite a deeper aliveness to flow through us. We do not really know what anybody else needs or what is truly right in their lives, but we can trust that there is a deeper wisdom that does know. We offer our attention and presence to fulfilling that deeper wisdom. We concentrate this experience to Wholeness, within us and around us. (pause) . . . .

3. Notice your breathing. Watch the breath as it flows in and out. Stay with this . . . effortlessly watching the unbroken wave of breath. First in . . . then turning . . . and out . . . then turning . . . and in . . . . (pause)

4. Become aware of the shift in awareness that occurs as you stay with the breathing. Keep watching the breath. If the breathing changes, let it. Don't try to control or regulate the breath, just watch it. Notice the breathing as if you were watching a wild animal; you don't want to create anything that might frighten it away. Let the touch of your awareness be very light, very subtle. (pause)

5. To help attune to the subtle quality aroused by gently noticing the breath, imagine that the center of your chest is porous and you are breathing in and out through it. Feel the

breath as it comes in and out through this fine, porous area . . . . *(pause)*

6. Become aware of what this feels like . . . As you breathe in through this space—the porous, transparent area in the mid-chest—become exquisitely receptive. The more receptive you are to the space . . . the more exquisitely and delicately receptive . . . the larger and more substantial the space becomes . . . . As you breathe out, relax utterly into this space, sink into it, dissolve into it . . . become the space. *(pause)* The receptive in-breath gathers energy to the space within awareness . . . it seems filled with subtle feeling, subtle presence. *(pause)* As you breathe out, surrender yourself into this space. By surrendering, you are merging into the space. Sense how the space is becoming more alive as you breathe out into it. *(pause)*

7. Extend this feeling by expanding the area of receptivity as you breathe in. Involve your whole upper body. *(pause)* It is as though the whole upper body were porous . . . transparent to the breath. *(pause)* Continue to let your awareness be gently and exquisitely receptive to this space as you breathe in and out through the whole upper body . . . the chest . . . the arms . . . the hands . . . . As you breathe out, actively fill the space generated by the exquisite sensitivity of the inhalation. *(pause)* . . . .

8. The breath itself has become something else . . . a vehicle for subtle feeling . . . subtle energy that is gathering and deepening within your awareness as you breathe. Stay with this awareness . . . go deeper into this subtle feeling of presence or energy. *(pause)* . . . Give yourself permission to become even more receptive to this subtle feeling . . . . Breathing out, sink into this feeling . . . merge into it . . . let go, utterly, into it . . . . Sense it becoming fuller, stronger, breath by breath. *(pause)* . . . .

9. Now extend this process through your whole body . . . as though the whole body has become, through the breath, a door to a larger space. *(pause)* . . . .

10. Now the quantum leap. Begin to extend this sense of

awareness outward, about one foot beyond the skin boundary. As before, become exquisitely receptive to this space as you inhale. The receptivity draws the energy of awareness to the space so that it becomes filled with a subtle presence . . . filled with a gentle energy. (*pause*) . . . As you breathe out, sense your own breath as a presence that fills this space. In this way, you are beginning to empower a field of energy around the body. Stay with this presence within and around the body. Let it get as deep as it can. (*pause*) . . . .

11. If you become aware of thoughts, or are distracted by them, allow your awareness of these thoughts to just relax. It doesn't matter what the content is. Imagine that your awareness has grabbed these thoughts firmly and that is why they are so strong. Now just let the grip relax; let your hand open; let the grasp of your awareness become softer and softer. Do not fight the thoughts; let them be. Just let the grasp of your awareness become softer and softer . . . . The thoughts or other distractions will change of themselves. Let them dissolve away like the mist off dry ice. Gently, return to the breath and the space within and around the body . . . . Gently return to the sense of this space . . . its subtle aliveness . . . subtle presence. (*pause*) . . . .

12. Now we will begin to transmute the quality of the embrace to a finer energy. To do so, our relationship to the moment must become even more surrendered and unconditional. Sense into the presence within and around you in which your partner is contained. Begin to offer this awareness to a higher potential.

As you breathe in, allow a sense of "yes." It is a yes to the moment, a yes to life (*pause*) . . . . Feel your heart melting with each yes. Feel it opening to embrace existence. (*pause*) . . . . With each breath, allow this to become a sense of celebration. (*pause*) . . . .

13. As you breathe in, become exquisitely sensitive to the depth, the fineness, the purity of yes. It is as though your whole being is becoming a living prayer. (*pause*) . . . . With each out-

breath, sense your awareness flowing out into this shared space, deepening it, adding energy and presence to it. *(pause)* . . . . Become totally open to the presence that is filling the space of awareness. As you breathe in, refine this presence by imaging it to be the purest energy, the finest love. *(pause)* . . . . The more receptive you become to it, the finer it becomes . . . and, as you again enter awareness with the exhalation, your breath delicately but actively merges with this awareness and empowers it . . . becomes fuller . . . more palpable. *(pause)* . . . .

14. Let the sense of celebration become as fine, as simple, as effortless as it can, breath by breath, moment by moment . . . . When self-consciousness returns, when awareness of the surroundings or of your partner as separate arises . . . celebrate this . . . say yes to this . . . let the awareness dissolve into the sense of presence . . . . Stay with this for awhile, exploring this space. *(Reader: At this point allow yourself to relax and stay quietly present while the partners continue in this space. There should be no more directions for five to ten minutes.)*

15. Now let this quality of awareness that you sense within and around you, extend to embrace the people on either side of you . . . . As you breathe in, become receptive to this larger space that includes them . . . as you breathe out, sense yourself filling this space, enriching and empowering it with the love of life. *(pause)* . . . .

16. *(Reader: If this exercise is occurring in order for the group to share energy with a specific person, read the following.)*

Now extend the field of awareness to include _____, She(he) is not separate, but within this field of refined awareness. Just include her(him) in the field of your awareness, a field that is simply celebrating life, right now. *(pause)* . . . . Let us stay quietly with this space . . . with each breath surrendering to the perfect love, the finest energy that we can sense and offer ourselves to. *(pause)* . . . .

17. If anyone feels moved to touch _____, just let your hand rest gently wherever you feel guided to touch. Let the energy flow through you and out your hand . . . . Again, you

are celebrating the wholeness of the moment in the presence of loved ones. There is nothing to do, nothing to force. Just be present. *(let this go on for ten minutes or so)*

18. Now, everyone please return to your seat and for the next few minutes let the breath and the energy that moves with it flow gently through you. Let your whole being be suffused in this gentle presence. Allow your whole being to feel restored, rested, and clear. *(pause for three minutes)*

19. Now we will conclude the sharing . . . . Gradually allow yourselves to return to normal awareness. Be clear about where you are and be sure that, if you are going to have to drive an automobile shortly, you have given yourself a clear instruction to return fully to normal consciousness.

20. Verbal sharing is now invited.

5 / The Medical Personnel

Prior to going to surgery or undergoing any medical procedure ask your physician, anaesthetist, nurses, and anyone else who will be involved with you to join you for a few minutes. Even five minutes is enough. It is not easy to get all of these people together at the same time, so you may be sharing with the nurses at a different time than with doctors. The best time is just before the procedure. Simply have them sit or stand quietly near you. Ask them to hold hands lightly as a symbol of the bond of humanness that unites us all. If you can do it yourself, just speak from your heart about what you are feeling and how you have consecrated yourself. Invite them to perform their finest work, and to be a vehicle not only for their technical skill, but for the love that can flow through them as they work. Let them know that, whatever the outcome, you are grateful. If you are unable to speak, then trust silence or invite someone to stand in for you who you feel can invoke the appropriate mood of love and reverence. After this invocation, invite all persons present to speak briefly if they have anything to say.

Commentary

The very way in which you do this, how it makes you feel, the response of your physician(s) and other health-care friends is the basis of this exercise.

Give to the people you request to join you the freedom to say yes or no. It doesn't matter. Whatever their response, observe your own reactions. No matter what they choose to do, explore remaining open and at peace. See if you can release the tendency to withdraw or condemn if they will not participate. See if you can explain why it is important to you and yet not force them in any way.

What we are aiming for here is a short period in which the basis of the healer/healed relationship is released into a larger context in which we are all just human beings. If the "patient" and the "health-care personnel" can touch this space together (a space in which we are all one in life), the medical procedure becomes something larger. It becomes a celebration of that Oneness. This kind of rapport automatically means that more energy will be available during the procedure. When there is greater communion between people, there is a greater flow of life force. Then the whole experience, and the outcome as well, are likely to be more fulfilling.

6 / Solo

Energy Embrace becomes a palpable sense of presence when shared between people, but the same kind of consciousness is possible in relationship to experience itself. This is an excellent state to explore when you are by yourself, especially when you feel alone and cut off from the world.

❀

Begin to follow the breath and the awareness progression as described in the first Energy Embrace exercise. Stay with the breathing until there is a subtle sense of presence within the body, as if your whole body were porous or transparent. *(pause)*

Now begin to extend this sense into the surrounding environment . . . . Keep your eyes open and become exquisitely receptive to the room you are in, the lighting, the shapes, colors, sounds and smells. Breathe into all of it. With each in-breath, become receptive to all of this as if you were breathing *through* it . . . . As you breathe out, let the air flow from you, gently and evenly . . . . Let the sense of the exhaling air join you to the space you perceive around you . . . . Let the sense of presence within you flow outward to merge into the external environment.

Open outward into the immediacy of the moment, despite any fear. It is all right to be afraid. But if fear or any other emotion is intense, gently hum into it; hum into the space in your body where the emotion feels the strongest. As the energy frees out of any intense emotion, you may feel strongly energized. Just keep letting go into the moment, breath by breath, extending your awareness until it fills the whole environment.

EPILOGUE: THE ULTIMATE HOSPITAL

There is the mystery of the oneness of God, that at whatever place I, a tiny bit, lay hold of it (life), I lay hold of the whole. And since all aspects of life are radiations of His being, so he who lives a moment in love to its very ground, in this lays hold of a tiny bit of the oneness of God, and holds the whole in his hands as if he had fulfilled it.

BAAL SHEM TOV (author's rendering)

THERE IS THE PRESUMPTION IN MEDICINE that it takes the scientific approach to human health. But the science in modern medicine is incomplete at best. The manipulation of biological systems is more a refinement of technology, based on a very mechanistic sense of ourselves, than something that truly increases our understanding of humanness. There is the unquestioned assumption that with suffi-

143

cient examination, particularly by manipulation of life functions in as many ways as possible, we will come to some ultimate understanding. Millions of dollars are given every day to research facilities throughout the world that are desperately trying to maneuver themselves into the spotlight by modifying biology to yield the next cure. Rarely is there a new idea or a new look at life and aliveness.

Is there any such thing as an isolated human organism? I suggest that the focus on the individual body as an organism— without simultaneous consideration of consciousness in general, and collective consciousness, in particular—represents the most confining and shortsighted aspect of modern medicine. At a gross level, we already understand this. For example, good sanitation saves more lives than all of modern medicine. Preventive medicine deals with finding the paths by which disease spread and then, through sanitary habits or isolation, limiting the spread. When something is found to be good for a number of people, it is then offered to everyone. In these primitive ways we are treating the whole to improve the individual, and incidentally acknowledging their inseparability. Now I am asking that we look much deeper, into the very structure of our consciousness, to observe how we meet life—how deeply we enter into the door of each moment. I am suggesting that we can access whole new levels of life force through the mystery of our relationship to life and, more specifically, our relationship to each other.

Before we can discuss greater aliveness we must ask, "What is my body and how do I know it?" In fact, medicine does not really deal with the body you and I know from direct experience. Rather, it deals with a body that is an object of mental reflection, a body that is isolated from its environment and cultural context. Because this is the case, and because we can point with our intellect to this object called "the body" and make infinite observations about it, we believe that the body, seen in this way, is real. However, only at one conceptual level is it real. Medicine does have some power over this level. But, when we look at our bodies from another level of awareness, we realize that we "know" the body only subjectively. We sense our body; we also see it in the mirror. Yet at the deepest level of observation we are nothing but consciousness, continuously arising in the mind. Furthermore, the body we claim to know through subjective observation constantly changes as our energy or our psychic environment changes. It changes as we shift our beliefs, our behavior, our physical location, and our spiritual orientation—the quality in which our relationship to life and each other is consecrated.

I propose that, if we wish to start from a perspective of wholeness, we can no longer speak of an isolated human organism. A person walks into a doctor's office and says, "I have indigestion and a cough and my back hurts and . . . " will experience worsening or lessening of those symptoms depending on whom she or he is addressing. If it is a radiantly alive individual, the alteration in self-perception (not necessarily for the better in a subjective sense) can be quite dramatic.

I saw this clearly while practicing medicine. Some people came into our office with fevers, and, within five minutes of receiving a gentle shoulder massage from the nurse, or sitting with me, their fevers diminished. Now, it is well known that the physician functions as a placebo, but we are not speaking here of the placebo effect as it is commonly understood. We are making the radical statement that all human beings are continuously interacting in a field of consciousness, with an uninterrupted positive or negative placebo effect. The origin of the word *placebo* is "to please"; it also implies mutual understanding. Mutual understanding suggests a dynamic of energetic communion where, by our coming together, we begin to define a new reality. It is this accord that is the greatest placebo. And the more our accord is consecrated in wholeness, the more profound the "reality" we create together.

The Ultimate Hospital presumes that life is an inseparable

whole. "Ultimate" does not suggest an end-point, but a process consecrated to a higher, as yet unattempted, synthesis of science and consciousness. Within a milieu consecrated to aliveness and the fullness of consciousness, the health-care techniques and procedures are no longer ends in themselves, but scaffolds for a way of coming together to produce the greatest aliveness out of the sheer adventure of life!

Imagine entering a hospital where, several times each day, the staff meditates and celebrates with all patients who are able to participate. They might sing, dance, hum or sit quietly in Energetic Embrace. Physical contact would be encouraged wherever possible. In these ways, the potential to heighten life-force energies would be constantly acknowledged, and we would be constantly exploring the miracle of relationship. Singing would be encouraged, and patients and staff would be welcome to break into spontaneous song, and through their songs, share themselves intimately and vulnerably. Imagine discovering that the nausea and fatigue of your chemotherapy treatment could be transmuted through communal song and celebration!

Imagine that all people would regard their work in such a hospital as inseparable from their private lives, that their home lives would be an extension of their work lives and vice versa. Thus they would not be dissipating their energies at home and diminishing the presence they can bring into their work. You would know that all people who share with you while you are in this hospital consider it a privilege. Imagine a staff that regards being well-rested and clear as their sacred duty. They know that this will enable them to meet you at a deeper level, and to touch fuller states of aliveness in themselves. Patients, staff and visitors would all be regarded as a resource relative to the group energy and included in every way possible.

Imagine the emergency room, surgical, and ward teams understanding how to tap their collective energy and thus create a high-energy milieu. Because everyone would be continuously exposed to higher energies, each person would be challenged to master his or her own personal process. Such a hospital might sound utopian, but in practice it would be a transformative cauldron demanding maturity and responsibility from everyone involved. The Ultimate Hospital would be a school for empowering radical aliveness and awakening higher human potential. Just by activating their hand energies, nurses, doctors, or orderlies could help relieve pain. Because trauma often makes people more energetically available, they become particularly open to energy transfer. In some instances hand energies may even replace local anaesthesia, and in others the heightened energy might reduce the requirement for drugs. People could be made comfortable and peaceful while maintaining or even heightening their alertness.

Furthermore, because people with different illnesses often have different energy dynamics, the Ultimate Hospital could explore the health benefits of bringing these people together. For instance, what happens when the openness of the schizophrenic energy field is brought onto the cancer ward?(9) What happens when elderly patients are brought into contact with children? The unique quality of old age, so valuable to youth, could be maximized, and seniors could experience a sense of worth in their lives once again.

Finally, it would be the responsibility of every person in the Ultimate Hosptial to explore the nature of the unique consciousness shift brought about by illness. In addition to rounds where the staff studies the patient's disease, there would be rounds where the patients teach the healthy about the consciousness that has emerged from their limitations. I believe it is essential that we learn, for instance, what it is like to need two hours in the morning to go to the bathroom and to prepare breakfast. A person with multiple sclerosis might teach this to the nondisabled, guiding them into this altered time frame. This allows the opportunity to creatively shift our perspective. It is not hard to imagine that such a slowed capacity to live and work might very well represent health in our breakneck, frenzied world. One of the great gifts of illness is the alteration of time, and we must learn to embrace it.

In the Ultimate Hospital, every medical procedure will involve energetic preparation and attunement among the patients' families and staff. Every day will start with physical conditioning of some kind—dancing or walking—for everyone who can participate, but especially for the staff. Without physical conditioning it is difficult to sustain a heightened energetic, and we tend to crystallize in confining levels of consciousness.

All this attention to the overall way of life does not for a moment imply neglect of traditional professional skills. Traditional medicine lifted to a higher energy is the primary service. Every health professional would be meticulously trained to adhere to the most rigorous standards of the conventional medical establishment. Nor am I suggesting a hospital with a dozen additional departments for alternative approaches. Since the Ultimate Hospital is based on relationships consecrated in Oneness, there is no separation between the traditional and non-traditional. The principles of aliveness unify all approaches.

❋

The Ultimate Hospital is the expression of a way of life that honors the mystery of transformation. It is a spiritual school in which it is a privilege to work, in which the patients give the gift of receiving and the staff receives the gift of giving. It is a place where healer and the healed can never be separated. It is an environment in which the untapped potential of consciousness is seen as the greatest resource, and where true health is not merely physical recovery but an increased capacity to love. Since a unified collective energy is the greatest force for empowering aliveness and a transformational shift in consciousness, it is the exploration of what this means and how it can be lived that is the heart of the Ultimate Hospital. There is no social or professional hierarchy based on education or skill, but rather a hierarchy of responsibility based on spiritual maturity and the capacity to tune the energy field so that all relationships reach their fullest potential. To this end, a maintenance person might have more authority than a doctor, for spiritual maturity is a product of self-knowledge, commitment, and surrender to a higher concept.

To be drawn toward the Ultimate Hospital means a genuine call from inner knowing. It is recognizing one's lover in the willingness to surrender one's life deeply and to risk living at the edge of the unknown. Each must understand that this life has nothing to do with achievement or attaining some new prize or skill. Each must have looked deeply enough into life to realize that every worldly motive is transient; that information, no matter how well-handled, does not bring security or control; that personal transformation is the greatest of life's adventures and that such transformation is impossible without a sense of the Divine and a community with which to share.

Hardly anyone emerging from our educational system has heard even a hint of this possibility. Furthermore, our socialization process does not demand the maturity the Ultimate Hospital would require. I thought that I was an adult when I finished training and began to practice medicine, but I wasn't. I had rudimentary mental skills and emotional mastery, and sufficient training to step into a socially defined role. But I was not an adult. I did not really know how to think, nor did I have any sense of Consciousness or of Love. I had always been sensitive, felt the pain of others and had been, in my own way, a teacher and a friend, but my social awareness did not extend beyond being conventionally responsible (so I could not be blamed) and trying to meet my own needs for companionship. I had no real sense of my own values or beliefs, and my feelings were a medley of reactions.

There was no sense of a deeper current or unifying principle. For all these reasons, I could not be called an adult, nor could most people, no matter what their age.

At this level of development, no one could make a commitment to the way of life required by the Ultimate Hospital, no matter how much they might be attracted by its ideals. They simply would not have the inner credentials. There must be some kind of opening, an inner refinement—perhaps brought about by a deep wounding, or by self-exploration that has turned the consecration toward the Divine, the Unknown. But consciousness is not expanded without cost and most people look at transformation as a desirable achievement without fully appreciating that the price is a process of difficult self-surrender and undoing. For truly, what we propose is a spiritual community whose skeleton is a medical facility, but whose flesh and blood is transformation of consciousness. Furthermore, since the basic ego structure and the development of career go hand in hand for most people, when we begin to awaken and realize that we have chosen a career unconsciously, there is a natural tendency to leave that career behind. The Ultimate Hospital is just as likely to free people from their careers in health care as it is to involve them more deeply in those careers! Such a career must be an affirmation of one's soul and not an idealistic fantasy.

I believe there are people longing for this adventure. Many health-care personnel are drawn to their careers because of underlying spiritual and social sensitivity. It is frequently these people who are driven out of the health-care field because the average hospital does not allow them to discover their full aliveness. It is getting harder and harder to fill nursing positions at modern hospitals because of the extreme regimentation of nurses' responsibilities: the pill pushing, the patient overload, the hierarchy of power that resides with doctors and supervisors, and, most important, the sense of not being allowed to meet the patients, spend time with them, and risk involvement. Besides drawing upon these people, the Ultimate Hospital would invite older, more seasoned individuals, who are naturally drawn to a transfomational way of life and involvement with people. These individuals might return to school for training if they knew it would be more than a way to program their participation in the world—that it would prepare them for entrance into a never-ending learning and growth process of the highest order.

One of the greatest illusions of our time is that we think we know what we are doing. This is particularly true in the health-care field. This myth must disappear from our health-care facilities if we are to invite truly mature people to work there and if we are going to allow a new level of aliveness. Being well-trained should not mean that we know what we are doing, even if we are eminently capable of repeating certain thoroughly memorized routines. Physicians have confessed to me that they often behave as though they know what they are doing, but when they make a choice during surgery, or adjust the electrolytes of a premature infant, they really have no assurance that their actions will produce positive results. Yet it is amazing how few people will ever acknowledge to themselves that, while they strive for excellence and competence in their work, the truth is they often don't know what they are doing. There are fewer still who can face this truth and, rather than seeking more knowledge or feeling inadequate, rest in the understanding that this is how it is. We must let our unknowing become a source of spontaneity, humor, and radiant presence.

When we act in the presumption of knowing, we are limiting the field of interaction. Our certainty is as much the statement of our own boundedness as it is the reflection of our knowledge. It is not that we should cease our pursuit of knowledge, but that we should persist in our appreciation of ignorance and the door it opens for us. This fundamental ignorance, which can never be overcome no matter how far science goes, will always invite a spiritual orientation to life, a renewed orientation toward the unknown, and a respect for the Unknowable.

The Ultimate Hospital is an invitation. The great experiment, the untried scientific thesis, is to act from our fundamental wholeness, to recognize that wholeness is not merely within ourselves, not something that can be attained, not some form of personal enlightenment or liberation, but rather is the basic condition of all life. We are spending billions to cure diseases without thinking to explore a way of life in which many of these diseases might not exist.

It is easier to fight disease than to live in a process of collective aliveness. It is easier to spend billions for health care — to develop a more powerful scanning device, a more potent chemotherapy, to blame the society, the government, the germs — than it is to engage in responsible, conscious association. It is not my intent to imply that the Ultimate Hospital would generate miraculous levels of energy that would cure all diseases. The application of scientific understanding through technology will be a major aspect of medical care now and for as long as I can envision. But if medicine is to be a truly scientific pursuit, then it must also create environments in which a sense of wholeness is presumed and all the relationships are consecrated in that wholeness. In such an environment, we may well begin to see more of what we truly are.

One real difficulty must be faced. The Ultimate Hospital cannot be implemented like a usual hospital. It must grow organically, as a tree grows organically, stage by stage. If someone were to give me fifty million dollars to develop such a hospital, perhaps I could inspire it, but money guarantees nothing in an adventure such as this. For at its heart, the Ultimate Hospital is people, and they can't just be hired; they must be ready to surrender utterly and to mature consciously together. This hospital is not a hospital, it is a spiritual body.

Finally, if the experiment of the Ultimate Hospital is possible, then a socially integrated, high-energy environment is also possible, and this has profound significance. As a rule, society organizes into energetic wholeness in times of crisis. For this reason, war often serves the purpose of profoundly energizing society, of accelerating transformation on a collective level, thereby fulfilling the natural imperative to grow in consciousness. Crisis is a limited mode of growth. The Ultimate Hospital transcends the crisis mode for empowering aliveness. Its aliveness resides in the process of surrender into the unknown and in impeccable commitment and will to conscious living and profound relationships that invoke transformation. It is committed to tapping the potential in life's natural moments of power (birth, illness, death) and love, through the profound energies of consecrated human community. Perhaps the Ultimate Hospital will be the living demonstration of a way of life that no longer requires war to empower transformation. If so, it is a model for the medicine our world vitally needs.

FOOTNOTES

(1) Much of this experience is reported and discussed in my book, *The I That Is We*, Celestial Arts: Berkeley, California, 1981.

(2) Moss, Richard. *Radical Aliveness*, Celestial Arts: Berkeley, California, available in 1986.

(3) Statistical data from the *Hospital Fact Book*, 1983.

(4) Moss, Richard, *The I That Is We*, Chapters 8 and 9.

(5) Suppression refers to the tendency of the brain to strategically eliminate one image, so that while the eye drifts, the person perceives only a single image. In my case, I could watch both images.

(6) Eliot, T.S., "The Four Quartets."

(7) With the danger of transfusion-caused diseases such as hepatitis and AIDS, the potential to heighten energy and decrease bleeding is of tremendous importance.

(8) Matthew 22:37-40.

(9) I discuss the relationship between schizophrenia and cancer in *The I That Is We* and *Radical Aliveness*. Briefly, schizophrenics have about one-fifth the incidence of cancer for the general public. My observations suggest that the psychic unboundedness of the schizophrenic is in part the basis for this difference. The instances of rapid healing following an A to A' shift (expansion of boundaries) tends to confirm this hypothesis. The suggestion that bringing certain schizophrenics and cancer patients together might be beneficial is a speculation that mutually enwholing induction might occur between them.

❁   ❁   ❁

Richard Moss, M.D., released the practice of medicine in 1976 and has since led workshops and conferences throughout the world. He is widely regarded as an inspirational teacher and master at awakening individuals into new dimensions of consciousness. His work bridges traditional medical, psychological and spiritual attitudes and goes into the direct experience of higher consciousness. He is a member of the American Holistic Medical Association and American College of Preventive Medicine.

He is married and enjoys rock climbing and tending the orchards of his home at the base of the eastern Sierras. He founded and directed the transformational community at Sky High Ranch for three years before moving to Lone Pine, California in 1984. Three Mountain Foundation, a nonprofit organization, provides conferences, lectures, tapes and other writings based on Dr. Moss's work.

❁   ❁   ❁

RELATED MATERIALS

THREE MOUNTAIN FOUNDATION

Three Mountain Foundation is a nonprofit organization which invites people into greater aliveness, health and wholeness. The foundation sponsors conferences and workshops for individuals, organizations, and hospitals, including the transformational conferences led by Richard Moss referred to in this book. Its books, tapes and magazine address all aspects of transformation. Based on the work of Richard Moss, the foundation is continuously unfolding in new directions. Its work is timeless and is the basis of a cultural and social evolution revealing new possibilities for life.

HOW SHALL I LIVE—SPECIAL TAPE SERIES

This three-cassette tape series was created to augment and complement the book *HOW SHALL I LIVE*. The interview with Dr. Moss and excerpts from two of his talks amplify the material presented in his book. Two inductions or exercises by Dr. Moss guide the listener through the energy embrace and help the listener to experience states of openness and aliveness. Like the book, this tape series is for the patient, family, friends, doctors, therapists—anyone involved in a health crisis or wishing to explore transformation.

$24.95 plus $1 postage and handling. California residents add 6% sales tax. Overseas add $5. U.S. funds only.

HOW SHALL I LIVE – SEMINARS

These workshops explore the concepts presented in the book and are for anyone involved with a health crisis. Through exercises and discussions, they provide the opportunity to experience expanded states of awareness. These seminars do not emphasize particular sets of exercises or techniques, but focus on developing an awareness of the energy that enables any technique to work. The workshops are designed to help people find new aliveness in all areas of life.

Contact Three Mountain Foundation for current schedule. Continuing education credit for nurses.

THE I THAT IS WE

Regarded as a definitive work on transformation, people from all over the world have expressed their appreciation for this book because it has confirmed and elucidated their experience and provided new possibilities for their lives. In this book Dr. Moss discusses individual and collective energy, and how group energies can be shared for transformation and healing. It is about the awakening to higher consciousness and the physical, psychological and spiritual aspects of transformation. (Celestial Arts, 1981)

$8.95 plus $1 postage and handling. California residents add 6% sales tax. Overseas plus $5. U.S. funds only.

RADICAL ALIVENESS

This book expands the theories presented in *HOW SHALL I LIVE*. Dr. Moss asks incisive questions about our personal approach to life and its relationship to our own health and society as a whole. He links our personal aliveness and willingness to embrace the fullness of life to the transformation of society. (To come from Celestial Arts, 1986)

AUDIO TAPES BY RICHARD MOSS

Talks covering all aspects of the transformational process are available on cassette tapes. These tapes have been heard throughout the world by those who are engaged in the exploration of consciousness. They are recommended by doctors, therapists, and ministers to assist individuals who are in crisis or transition. Each tape can bring the listener into heightened awareness.

Please contact Three Mountain Foundation for an updated list.

THE THIRD MOUNTAIN is a quarterly tape and magazine published by Three Mountain Foundation. The immediacy of the tape and magazine format is an ongoing forum on transformation, aliveness, and consciousness exploration.

Yearly subscription: $40 for tape and magazine. $15 for magazine alone. Canada and Mexico add $7. Overseas add $12. U.S. funds only.

For information about the work of Three Mountain Foundation contact the address below.

For books, tapes, and magazine, if not available in your local book store, send check or money order in U.S. funds to:

THREE MOUNTAIN FOUNDATION
P.O. BOX 1180
LONE PINE, CA 93545
(619) 876-4702